The Fleet Without A Friend

John Vader

NEW ENGLISH LIBRARY
TIMES MIRROR

To those intrepid French navigators
David, Hermia and Amanda

First published in Great Britain by New English Library in 1971
© 1971 by John Vader

*

FIRST NEL PAPERBACK EDITION FEBRUARY 1973
Reprinted May 1973

*

NEL Books are published by
New English Library Limited from Barnard's Inn, Holborn, London E.C.1.
Made and printed in Great Britain by C. Nicholls & Company Ltd.

450012263

THE FLEET WITHOUT A FRIEND

CONTENTS

Chapter 1

INTRODUCTION

AT the beginning of June in that disastrous year of 1940 the most ridiculous possibility in any naval situation would be that closely allied British and French warships would open fire on each other.

At the beginning of July the ridiculous happened: British battleships fired salvo after salvo of 15-inch shells into the North African port of Mers-el-Kebir at Oran where four French battleships, caught like sitting ducks, were slowly moving out to face the challenge.

To the Royal Navy it was a shameful action; to America and the rest of the world it was an indication that Britain was fighting back, and if the French were quitting the struggle against Germany they too would be attacked for risking the loss of their warships to the enemy. But was the attack on an old friend worthwhile? In this story of the French Navy in the Second World War it is important to follow Winston Churchill's attitudes, his speeches and decisions, for he influenced and expressed the mood of the British War Cabinet and the people, if not that of the Royal Navy and its senior admirals.

It had as much to do with Winston Churchill as with anyone else, with his sense of honour regarding Britain's alliance with France and his facing up to the reality of the desperate situation when German armoured columns broke through French defences north of the Maginot Line: France must honour her alliance and continue to fight, to deny the enemy any material assistance. In his first broadcast as Prime Minister he asked the British people to "arm yourselves, and be ye men of valour . . ." and was readily accepted as a strong fighting leader. He made that broadcast on 19th May, 1940, two days after the Germans had entered Brussels, on the day General Weygand took command of the French forces and the day the enemy captured St. Quentin.

Although he spoke of "invincible confidence in the French Army and its leaders," and expected the battle in France to abate its force, he was aware of the conquering might of German armour and air forces, and the need for Britain and France to remain united in purpose:

"I have received from the Chiefs of the French Republic, and in particular from its indomitable Prime Minister, M. Reynaud, the most sacred pledges that whatever happens they will fight on to the end, be it bitter or be it glorious. Nay, if we fight to the end, it can only be glorious."

Brave words and strong pledges, but premiers can only speak while they are Prime Ministers, for their governments and military leaders, and cannot always pass their honour to successors, as M. Reynaud discovered.

Also in his speech on that Trinity Sunday, Churchill spoke of his faith in the Alliance:

"This is one of the most awe-inspiring periods in the long history of France and Britain. It is also beyond doubt the most sublime. Side by side, unaided except by their kith and kin in the great Dominions and by the wide Empires which rest beneath their shield – side by side, the British and French peoples have advanced to rescue not only Europe but mankind from the foulest and most soul-destroying tyranny which has darkened and stained the pages of history. Behind them – behind us – behind the armies and fleets of Britain and France – gather a group of shattered States and bludgeoned races ... upon all of whom the long night of barbarism will descend, unbroken even by a star of hope unless we conquer, as conquer we must; as conquer we shall." One could readily see flags unfurling and fluttering across the lands where the sun never sank, and that loyalty

8

between France and Britain would last forever, no matter what trials of honour they may have to endure.

The armies and fleets of Britain and France, not yet properly tested in this second modern war against Germany, were the hope of freedom for western Europe; yet within a few days, by 24 May, the Germans had reached Calais and were besieging the ancient citadel; and on the 29th Dunkirk became the last major British defensive area in France, an evacuation point for the British Expeditionary Force and for the remnants of General Prioux's Army which had fought its way out after being cut off in Flanders. Before the evacuation began, Churchill feared that he might have to announce that only 20,000 or 30,000 men might be saved. The evacuation from Dunkirk was a glorious epic, made feasible by Goering's insistence on using his air force to destroy the rescuing ships and annihilate the Allied army – thus freeing the panzers for other work – and by the determined defence made by Royal Air Force fighters. Again the two Navies were to work as one.

Within the space of two weeks the war against Germany had changed from a battle to save France to an immediate threat of invasion of Britain, a Britain that had already lost over 30,000 men and enormous quantities of material – most of her armour and transport and nearly one thousand guns. In the House of Commons, on 4 June, Churchill outlined the grim events and the country's situation, and again repeated his faith in her Ally:

"The British Empire and the French Republic, linked together in their cause and in their need, will defend to the death their native soil, aiding each other like good comrades to the utmost of their strength."

And, foreseeing the lonely struggle that lay ahead, he finished his speech with those stirring words which gave so much tonic to the determination of his countrymen to resist invasion:

"We shall go on to the end, we shall fight in France, we

shall fight on the seas and oceans, we shall fight with growing confidence and growing strength in the air, we shall defend our island, whatever the cost may be, we shall fight on the beaches, we shall fight on the landing grounds, we shall fight in the fields and in the streets, we shall fight in the hills; we shall never surrender, and even if, which I do not for a moment believe, this island or a large part of it were subjugated and starving, then our Empire beyond the seas, armed and guarded by the British Fleet, would carry on the struggle, until, in God's good time, the new world, with all its power and might, steps forth to the rescue and liberation of the old."

A small but useful link would be retained with some men from the French Republic – and the Isles would be armed, and guarded by the British Fleet, without, however, the expected assistance of the bulk of the French Fleet: the political changes in a defeated France were to increase the danger of invasion and threaten the strength of the Royal Navy.

*

Antoine de Saint-Exupéry wrote, in *Flight to Arras*, that in the spring of 1940 everybody was repeating an ancient French saw – "France is always saved at the eleventh hour by a miracle" – while the pilots were facing their own particular problem of guns and controls freezing up because of poor design and incorrect lubricant. There was a reason for the eleventh hour miracle, he believed:

"It used to happen occasionally that the beautiful administration machine would break down and everybody would agree that it could not be repaired. For want of better, men would be substituted for the machine. And men would save France.

"If a bomb had reduced the Air Ministry to ashes, a corporal – any corporal at all – would have been summoned, and the government would have said to him, 'You are ordered to see that the controls are thawed out. You have full authority. It's up to you. But if they are still freezing up two weeks from now on you go to prison.'

"The controls would perhaps have been thawed out."

By 1940 the world's great bureaucracies were, after being disrupted by the Depression, building up to their pre-1914 glory – although railway stationmasters may never have regained the same air and appearance of admirals – and the French bureaucracy was the fussiest, slowest and most unproductive of them all. Even today in 1971, some small-town post offices give the impression that the PTT organization has rushed headlong from the Middle Ages to 1925, particularly when Madame behind the counter weighs twelve post cards individually, and all of them identical.

The French Navy was administered by a beautiful machine, highly disciplined and perhaps inspired by some of the modern equipment introduced in the Thirties. Two outstanding bureaucrats, Ministers of the Navy Georges Leygues and Francois Piétri, contributed their intelligence, energy and influence, and two very able and efficient admirals, Violette and Durand-Viel, guided the post-First War renovation towards a modernization which produced the fastest destroyers in the world. In 1937, Admiral Francois Darlan was appointed head of the French Fleet, establishing more firmly the already strong discipline and loyalty to its oaths that were to interfere with the reason for its existence: to fight France's enemies.

Actually, the French Fleet spent more time being tied up – if not scuttled – than fighting during the Second World War, and was actually the weapon – the "eleventh hour miracle" – which gave France something on which to bargain with the barbarians who, for the third time in seventy years, invaded across her flat plains in the north, this time continuing to the coast and reducing France to a "State" on the Mediterranean and only half its former area. Darlan was one of the perpetrators of the "miracle" and one sup-

11

poses from the information now available that he believed the Germans would win the war; he certainly showed no inclination to back Britain when France was collapsing, merely promising to scuttle the Fleet if the Germans attempted to grab it.

For Englishmen and Frenchmen, unfortunately still too many, there is a mythical haze hanging over the Channel which changes their mental vision when they try to look through at each other. There is the graduate girl who says "I think the French super but darling you know we've always hated each other," and there's the aged-one in Villeréal still mumbling about how awful it was that the British were boss in the area in the 13th century. Because Darlan's great-grandfather fought at Waterloo, Churchill supposed Darlan to be "one of those good Frenchmen who hate England." A pity the French admirals were not all from the South, for then there would have been rugby football to strengthen the alliance. Such days of ignorance and petty bias are fortunately rapidly passing. Unfortunately, think his historians, when Darlan was Chief of the Naval General Staff in 1937 he attended the Coronation of King George VI: Darlan's permanent rank then was merely Vice Admiral and he was placed behind a pillar in the Abbey, with a Chinese full admiral in a more forward position as protocol demanded. Darlan was, they say, upset. To make sure of a good seat for future coronations he had himself elevated to Admiral of the Fleet on his return to Paris, the rank he retained until his end. That slight had little, if anything, to do with his future actions.

Admiral Darlan was to become the most hated Frenchman in 1940, but if another French admiral had been in his position it may well have been a similar result because of influence from politicians like Laval and the influence of Marshal Pétain, and because of discipline. There were others to blame on both sides of the old Alliance for some of the enormous troubles which beset France and which, in October, caused the French Ambassador in Madrid to appeal to His Majesty's Ambassador there: if the French Government was not to be driven entirely into German hands, Great Britain must let supplies pass from French colonies to the Occupied Zone, and France would guarantee, to the extent of again confronting the Germans and transferring the Government to Morocco, that the supplies would be used only by Frenchmen.

That such an appeal should have to be made may seem strange in the light of previous events in the French Navy's action at sea and its later participation beside the Allies in European waters, and against the Japanese, but of all naval history the French Navy's is most unique, and deserves a more sympathetic reading than the biased propaganda handed out during the critical years of the war and at the post-war trials of French admirals.

Chapter 2

THE FRENCH NAVY

HONOUR, Country, Valour and Discipline were four gilded words displayed on quarterdecks of all French warships, four virtues which were to strand the Navy without an ally from June, 1940 to the end of 1942. Before then, the Navy lived up to those virtues and used its strength effectively in the opening rounds of the war.

In August, 1939, the last reserves were called up to fill the 160,000 places in the fleets and shore establishments, the Navy was placed on a war footing and a Franco-British signal code was brought out of its security vault.

Aircraft carriers were not considered by the French to be of great importance, in fact all navies in those days – including the Japanese – believed that the battleship was the number-one weapon. The 1927 model *Béarn* was France's only carrier, although another had been developed as far as the keel and part of the hull, before the armistice; and she had nine battleships and two uncompleted – *Jean Bart* and *Clemenceau*, the former floating and the latter in the Landévennec yards where it was bombed by the RAF in 1942.

The oldest battleships were *Condorcet* (1909), a training ship, three other pre-1914 models – *Courbet*, which became an anti-aircraft battery before ending as a breakwater, *Océan*, a German navy target ship, and *Paris*, an accommodation ship – and three 1919–1920 models, *Bretagne, Lorraine* and *Provence* which were refitted, re-boilered and equipped with more guns during the 'Thirties. The last three were of 22,000 tons, could make 21 knots and cruise 3,500 miles. *Lorraine* had eight, the others ten 340mm (13.4-inch) main armament.

Next in age were the two battlecruisers *Dunkerque* and *Strasbourg*, sleekly elegant with their long foredeck where all their main armament was stacked in two turrets of four guns, each of 330mm calibre; centre and aft were sixteen 130mm, twelve of which were also in four-gun turrets. These ships were of 26,500 tons displacement and had a radius of operation up to 7,500 miles at 15 knots. Both were scuttled at Toulon, *Strasbourg* was raised by the Italians and later bombed by Allied aircraft. The last active battleship, *Richelieu*, was almost completed in 1940; she displaced 35,000 tons, could make 30 knots and her longest radius was 5,500 miles at 18 knots carrying 6,796 tons of fuel oil; she too carried all her strength in front – two four-gun turrets firing 380mm (15-inch) shells – and her secondary armament in three-gun turrets, firing 152mm (6-inch) shells from fifteen guns. The *Jean Bart* did not get her one turret firing until 1942.

The modern French battleships would have been more than a match for Germany's pocket battleships had they ever been tested. Perhaps a greater threat to Germany's fleet were fast French destroyers, especially the *contre-torpilleurs*, the large or "super" destroyers, the heaviest of which were really light cruisers: *Mogador* and *Volta*, destined for the Toulon scrapheap, were almost 3,000-tonners, mounting eight 5.5-inch guns, and with top speeds of 43 knots averaged during 8 hours.

L'Audacieux, Le Fantasque, L'Indomptable, Le Malin, Le Terrible and *Le Triomphant*, of 2,600 tons displacement, were almost as fast and were built some three years earlier – 1933 and 1934. In the "2,100-tonnes" and "2,400-tonnes" classes were another twenty-four heavy destroyers, and there were another 38 ordinary destroyers. In a forseeable long war the Allied naval planners leaned heavily on the presence of French destroyers in the Mediterranean and the northern approaches, while the cruisers – twenty-two of them – would have been invaluable as escorts

15

on the long communication routes to the United States.

With main armament ranging from 5-inch to 8-inch, the cruisers were mostly old, but refitted to a high enough standard for 1940. The 8-inch-gunned *Algérie* was launched in 1932 and she could average 30 knots on only 75 per cent of her 66,000 SHP turbines; she displaced 10,000 tons. The *Emile Bertin*, 5,886 tons, was the model for six larger cruisers also built in the mid-'Thirties and the last to go into service before war broke out. There were numerous smaller craft, ranging from the "1,000-tonnes" class torpedo boats down to MTB's and minesweepers. And there were 71 submarines and 1 "submarine cruiser" – the *Surcouf*, the largest submarine vessel in the world, mounting two 8-inch guns, displacing 2,880 tons, and having a cruising range of 10,000 miles at 10 knots surfaced.

Surcouf was what the Germans really should have built for their raids against merchant ships. The submarine could send a 260-lb shell 30,000 yards less than three minutes after surfacing; her torpedoes were designed for close firing at merchantmen; she could cruise for ninety days and could accommodate 40 prisoners in comfort, more in discomfort. Her measurements were $361 \times 29\frac{1}{2} \times 23\frac{3}{4}$ feet in which 118 crew were accommodated. It is just as well the enemy did not get her or build replicas, for two 8-inch guns emerging from the sea, without warning and possibly without being seen, were a most formidable and frightening weapon that could have been used not only against shipping but devastatingly against towns also.

These warships of the French Navy added up to a force always included as a powerful element in all pre-war Allied planning – at least in Franco-British planning made during the rise of Nazi politicians and after Mussolini's unchecked (by the Allies) invasion of Abyssinia, the invasion Hitler saw as an example of the temerity of Britain and France when confronted by a *fait-accompli* no matter how contrary to past conventions and treaties. And France's naval bases in the Mediterranean, added to Britain's at Gibraltar, Malta and Alexandria, could have – would have – been factors to keep Mussolini's ambitions within reason; however that fool did not know when he was well off and was not really needed in the war by anyone.

That the coming war at sea was to be as ruthless as in the First War was evident when, under direct orders from the Nazi leaders, a U-boat torpedoed the British liner *Athenia* on the day war was declared, the day Neville Chamberlain appointed Churchill First Lord of the Admiralty. The presence of the battleships *Strasbourg* and *Dunkerque* at this time restricted the enemy's capital ships from coming down into the busy sealanes. *Dunkerque* safely escorted Canadian troops destined for France and that ship, *Lorraine* and the aircraft carrier *Béarn* transported several hundred tons of gold to Canada and the United States for safekeeping. The *Emile Bertin* took another 300 tons and diverted to Martinique when the armistice crisis arose.

During the first few months of 1940 the war was fought mostly at sea, against surface raiders and occasional sorties by the *Scharnhorst, Gneisnau, Deutschland* and *Graf Spee*, the latter being scuttled when cornered in the Rio de la Plata by two British cruisers. A dozen submarines operated with the Royal Navy and a minelaying sub also went into operations in the North Sea. Already the Allied merchant fleet was suffering from surface and submarine attack, and in one week 600,000 tons were sunk by German magnetic mines in the Channel and North Sea. That November week of 1939 demonstrated that if Britain ever had to fight Germany without the assistance of the French Fleet she would be in a highly vulnerable position; much worse, of course, if Italy were to enter the war, necessitating the maintenance of strong naval forces in the Mediterranean for convoy and defence duties.

There was nothing to worry about, then. Admiral Darlan's fleets were doing good work everywhere and willingly sent units to join the Royal Navy for the diversionary operations in Norway.

Russia invaded Finland, as it was jackal-time for Russia and Germany who had just divided Poland, and the Allied War Council sent the Finns aircraft and guns – and promised an expeditionary force which they hoped would be able to travel through Norway and Sweden. By March the Finns were overwhelmed by the huge Russian juggernaut and in April the Germans landed in Norway ahead of the Allies, setting the scene for two small naval battles – at Narvik.

Before these events came to pass, the British historian Captain (later Sir Basil) Liddell Hart said of his country's prospects in a possible war that "It would be folly to develop any effort on land which could weaken our sea power or air power." That advice was ignored on several occasions, the most disastrous being when Wavell, who had the capacity to push the Italians out of North Africa early in 1941, was ordered to split his forces and send his best troops to Greece and Crete where not only good soldiers were killed or captured, valuable ships also were lost. Closer to home, loss of sea power was possible in Norwegian waters, and loss of air power in France was a fact that forced Air Marshal Dowding to call a halt to Churchill's promises of more fighters during the Battle of France.

It was "too little too late" as usual in those days, made more indefinite by the Finnish collapse. At first the 12,500 French force was told to stand down, then ordered back into readiness and they landed in Norway on 20th April, a few days after the British and eleven days after the Germans had invaded Norway and Denmark. For France there would only be another two months of war before she too was forced to sign an armistice with Germany. It was too late to prevent the enemy from winning his outlets to the North Atlantic but the Norwegian campaign went ahead anyway.

First there was extensive mining of Norwegian waters, an occupation that went on for many tedious months when the fjords became havens for German warships. On the 8th, the German battlecruiser *Hipper* sank the destroyer *Glowworm* and the following day, when the Germans were on their way to the first push of the war in the west, the *Renown* almost brought *Scharnhorst* and *Gneisnau* to battle. The sanguinary British General Sir Adrian Carton de Wiart wrote of a later event:

"As day was breaking the Germans spotted us leaving the fjord and bombed us heavily. We lost the *Afridi* and a French destroyer and I lost my chance of being sunk. Having known the *Afridi* so well I asked to go on board, but had been told she was not coming in that night. When I found that she had come in after all I asked again to go in her, only to be told that my kit had been put on the *York* and it would be best for me to go in her instead. I did, and missed a very great experience (!) Unfortunately the wounded from the French destroyer had been put aboard the *Afridi* and nearly all of them were drowned." That unpleasant incident which aroused in de Wiart so much envy occurred during the evacuation; the French ship being the heavy destroyer *Bison* whose survivors were almost wrecked a third time. The air attacks that sank the two ships made naval operations in those waters a nightmare.

Earlier in the campaign the Norwegian sailors did quite well for themselves when the mine-layer *Olav Trggvason* severely damaged the light cruiser *Emden*, forced a destroyer to wreck itself on the shore and sank an enemy minesweeper. From the fortress of Oscarborg naval gunners fired on the German cruiser *Blücher* and while she engaged them in turn the fortress men fired torpedoes which sank the enemy ship. Those events took place in Oslo Fjord not long before German troops entered the capital to be greeted by Quisling's followers.

Fortress fire set alight to the cruiser *Königsberg* at Bergen, lighting the way for British Fleet Air Arm dive-bombers to finish her off. The next German to go down was the cruiser *Karlsruhe*, torpedoed by a British submarine. The Germans had suffered severely in ships they could not afford to lose, but the prize was probably worth it. Now they had the airfields, the small Norwegian navy was out of the fight, and the Allies were in a precarious position with their delayed invasion.

On the 10th, British mine-laying destroyers attacked a German flotilla in Narvik harbour, the port at the top of Norway. The odds were on the German side – with eight more heavily armed destroyers than the Royal Navy's five – and although *Hunter* was sunk and *Hardy* went aground, three of the enemy were set on fire, one was sunk and several supply ships were destroyed. Three days later the British returned to finish the job. Vice-Admiral Whitworth sailed the battleship *Warspite* to Narvik harbour, leading avenging destroyers and together they sank seven German destroyers, bringing the total of enemy shipping sunk to over 100,000 tons. That was a little like shooting sitting ducks, at Narvik harbour, but it was a good little morale-booster that all navies require to keep their pecker up. The Germans had had their victories, the most dramatic and morale boosting being U-47's remarkable penetration of the submarine defences at Scapa Flow to sink the mighty *Royal Oak*, on 14th October, 1939.

The French Navy did not enjoy any spectacular battles but plodded on with excellent convoy and support work. Under constant bombing attacks the cruiser *Emile Bertin* and auxiliary cruisers *El Djezair*, *El Mansour* and *El Kantara* took in men and supplies, and when the obviously impossible situation became intolerable, they took them out again. In charge of the French ships at Norway, Admiral Derrien flew his flag from the *Montcalm*. At Narvik, French troops under General Béthouart caused heavy casualties among the Germans as they drove them back, a gesture as it turned out, for Norway was evacuated the following day.

Meanwhile, in France the Germans had *not* attempted to make a frontal assault against the Maginot Line – as the Allies had hoped – but had gone down through the Low Countries and were compressing some half-a-million French and British troops towards that part of France which was closest to Britain. From Norway, some French troops were taken back to Britain, where with other French troops in reserve they remained until France fell.

In their history of the French Navy, Auphan and Mordal had this to say on Allied collaboration at sea during these early days:

"Never in history had there been more cordial relations than those established in the battle area of the sea off Norway. Not merely was this collaboration in the technical field, but the far more important field of human relations – the spirit of *camaraderie* between the French officers and their brethren of the Royal Navy. Whether they sailed with the Home Fleet on escort duty off the fjords of Norway, French and British ships, side by side, learned to sustain and to parry the fierce attacks of Germany's formidable Air Force." Some of the successful collaboration was the result of the quality of the liaison officers exchanged between the navies.

The *Kriegsmarine* too was formidable, less so after the Norway campaign where the *Scharnhorst* and *Gneisnau* were damaged and other casualties were inflicted on 3 cruisers, 10 destroyers, 4 submarines, a training ship and 10 smaller vessels. France lost the *Bison* and also during that period another heavy destroyer, the *Maillé-Brézé* was destroyed by the explosion of one of its torpedoes while stationed at Greenock.

*

Germany invaded the Low Countries on 10th May with a surprising use of airborne troops who effected a major coup when they captured the fort of Eben-Emael: nobody had bothered to move obstacles to the flat areas near the fort where gliders could land, nor had they mounted a strong array of anti-aircraft guns on the buildings. Everyone had talked about airborne troops which the major nations had used on exercises. The dawn invasion of Belgium continued with strength and ruthlessness, and while the Allied military commanders thought or dreamed of modern military tactics the Germans used them with devastating effect. And the Germans were war-keen, having been brainwashed for battle, while the majority of Allied soldiers – the reserves in particular – were not.

A German who took part in the attack on the fort later stated that "the storming of Eben-Emael was the first sapper attack ever made from the air. That it was successful is due to the efficiency and enthusiasm of the parachute sappers, using new weapons and new means of transport, aided by careful preparation, the participation of the Luftwaffe, and clear conditions of command." His criticism of the Belgians also applied to many French reservists: ". . . in spite of all preparations, the Belgian soldiers did not believe in the war, and, furthermore, what happened at Eben-Emael was typical of the whole 18-day campaign. Morale in Belgium had been weakened by neutralistic politics, and an ill-prepared army fought badly because it was badly led. For the most part it lacked the will to fight."

One could understand a small Belgian Army not being prepared or willing to fight against the overwhelming odds of a German armour-air-infantry attack; the Danes surrendered more readily because they had dropped out of any arms race and were virtually defenceless. The Low Countries' fields were ideal for the enemy to choose his first battle while Allied might stood about the Maginot Line, waiting to do their laundry when they reached the Siegfried Line – which they did, in 1944. Humanely, the King of the Belgians ordered his armourless twenty-three divisions to lay down their arms.

The Allies then had a combined air force about half the size of Germany's. On the ground, the Germans had ten armoured divisions against three French and part of one British, 118 infantry divisions against 63 French and 10 British, and the motorised divisions were about equal, except that the Germans had the advantage of total war-liking or conquer-madness induced into their systems. France's greatest handicap was the old disease of super-bureaucracy with too many false images at the top. At sea, all three navies were at tip-top condition, morale and efficiency in the highest traditions of sailors, but for the time being Hitler was not even concerned with developing a larger submarine fleet nor had his astrologist told him that he might need a hundred fast destroyers to carry an invasion force to the shores of England.

This is a chronology of the Blitzkrieg in the West, summarising what happened next:

May 12/15: German armour penetrates the French line near Sedan and begins its thrust to the coast.

May 14: The German bomber force attacks Rotterdam in a demonstration of ruthless strength, inflicting on the city's innocent civilians 30,000 casualties.

May 15: In the first major tank-versus-tank battle of the war Rommel's armour defeat French armour near Philippeville; General Reinhardt's armour advance thirty-seven miles west of the Meuse; then the Germans complete their breakthrough at Sedan; in the north Holland is forced to capitulate.

May 16: Retreat to the Schelde river is ordered by General Billotte.

May 18: St. Quentin, half-way from Sedan to the Channel, falls to a German armoured force led by General Kleist who then leads his force to take Péronne; Antwerp is occupied.

May 19: General Weygand is appointed Commander-in-Chief of all Allied forces in France.

May 20: The old Somme battlefield is reached by the invaders; the Allied force in the north is cut off when Kleist continues his drive and breaks through to the Channel near Abbéville.

May 21: British and French counterattack at Arras while the Germans claim that the French 9th Army is defeated.

May 23: German tanks and infantry reach Boulogne.

May 25: Allied troops are cut off and surrounded on the French coast in the Pas-de-Calais.

May 26: The evacuation of Allied troops at Dunkirk begins as Operation Dynamo is announced.

Militarily, the rot that had set in throughout France emanated from the leaders, soldiers and politicians; and if not rot then a sickness of conspiracy, jealousy and over-ambition in the Navy's command was to become evident after the land battles were lost, losses which were also to have an adverse effect on the Navy when so many of its ships and squadron commanders were given an opportunity to make up their own minds to continue the fight or go home. The historian Alistair Horne observed that the French army was "notably deficient in that all-important intangible – *morale*," a deficiency he briefly summarised as stemming from the "memories of Verdun and the 1,500,000 dead of the First World War" that weighed heavily on all ranks, the "sapping effects of the *Front Populaire*, appeasement, Hitler's bloodless victories, and the appallingly speedy smashing-up of Poland" that had left their mark, "as had the lethargy of the months of the 'Phoney War' itself."

The narrow dogmatism of the Pétain school of thought was a fatal factor in the fall of France, almost as fatal as

24

allowing the Germans to begin rearming in 1936, and not stopping Mussolini when he did his Caesar bit in Africa.

A French general added booze as a cause: ". . . we must add the pernicious effect of drink, this cancerous growth which gnaws at the lifeblood of the country . . . special rooms had to be prepared, euphemistically known as 'dis-ethylation rooms'!" The rooms were in railway stations used by troops returning from leave – they were not boozing in action but they, and their officers, may have drunk too much pernod on their evenings off in cafés. Also, there was too much leave during the "Phoney War" of inaction, so much that when the Germans caught them off guard there were several generals and thousands of officers and men away from their units. And poor old Gamelin was still living in the First War, and when Weygand – also aged but wiry and alert – took over, the new spark of activity at GHQ was too late.

Chapter 3

EVACUATION AT DUNKIRK

THE "conclusions" – as they are termed – recorded during British War Cabinet meetings in 1940, kept secret until they were released in January, 1971, are a cool summation of the conversations and decisions made by leaders of the two major political parties and heads of the services. After Neville Chamberlain's odd speech about Hitler having "missed the bus", made not long before Hitler's hordes proved him so very wrong, the Prime Minister resigned and Churchill replaced him.

The new Prime Minister took office on 10th May, and as a skilled naval administrator (he was First Lord of the Admiralty during part of World War One) he was fully aware of the position at sea. In 1939 a plan in three parts was formulated on the assumption that if war broke out it would be fought from the beginning against both Germany and Italy; the first part was concerned with defence of trade in British waters and the Atlantic approaches, the second was to contain the Italians and defend trade in the Mediterranean and the trade routes at either end, and the third was the blockade of the enemy. The Home Fleet based its main strength in Scotland with other forces under commands with headquarters at Plymouth, Portsmouth, the Nore and Rosyth; in the Mediterranean, the Gibraltar Straits and the Red Sea were areas of blockade supervision – as well as the natural barrier of the Suez Canal – and from Alexandria the Royal Navy dominated the eastern basin of the Sea while the French Navy dominated the western basin.

'"Fighting methods will never fail to be employed *merely because some international regulations are opposed to them*," was part of the German battle instructions. Before the outbreak of hostilities, the *Graf Spee* and the other pocket-battleship *Deutschland* went out with their tankers to the North Sea, undetected, and ocean-going U-Boats and minelaying submarines also went to their war stations in the Atlantic and mining-areas off the Channel ports. These moves were made following instructions set out in May, 1939: nuisance operations in the North Sea to bring large British forces into employment, and attack on trade in the Atlantic. At this stage only about twenty to twenty-five U-boats were operating at one time and Germany had not started its large U-boat building programme.

A weakness in Britain's Navy was the lack of long-range destroyers for escort work in the Atlantic, a lack which could be made up by French destroyers with their excellent range and speed, and it wasn't for another year that Britain could provide an escort of small warships right across the Atlantic; until then most convoys were forced to split up 300 miles west of Britain. While engaged on anti-submarine work the aircraft carrier *Courageous* was sunk and the *Ark Royal* survived a near-miss. In the first four months of the war U-boats had sunk 2,600,000 tons of shipping; mines, bombers, raiders and E-boats had sunk another 1,915,000 tons. The magnetic mine, one of Hitler's "secret weapons" caused the loss of 180,000 tons of shipping before a mine was picked up intact and unscrewed to reveal its secret, and a countering "degausing mantle" was fitted to ships.

Although Britain lost in a short time a battleship, an aircraft carrier, a cruiser and a few destroyers, she was only slightly weakened at sea. More serious was the danger to France once the Germans made their move. A couple of notable safety measures were the arrival of a cruiser, two destroyers, nine submarines and a minelayer of the Dutch Navy at Falmouth, and, earlier – on 28th March – an agreement between France and Britain *not to conclude peace separately*.

*

27

The more interesting "conclusions" reached at the secret War Cabinet meetings when French matters were discussed can be set down in their chronological order:

May 20: M. Deladier informed the British Ambassador, Sir Ronald Cameron, that he was turning over in his mind the possibility of opening negotiations with Italy and to make concessions immediately to Mussolini's demands. The Ambassador had done his best to discourage this idea.

Previously, M. Reynaud had suggested to the Briton that the best way to deal with Italy was to hit her first, and hit hard.

May 26: A piece of important gossip was picked up from the Chamberlain of Queen Ena (of Spain) who was informed by a highly placed Falangist that it was the Germans' plan that Italy should immediately offer a separate peace to France, on the basis that she kept her present European frontiers, while Italy received Tunis, Spain received Gibraltar and French Morocco, and France was to stand aside while Germany proceeded to blockade and invade England which, the Germans were convinced, they could readily achieve. The offer would be accompanied by an ultimatum that Italy would attack if it were not accepted.

May 30: There was never any question of leaving the French behind at Dunkirk. On the 29th, Churchill sent these letters, quoted in the secret "conclusions" and also quoted in historian Churchill's *The Second World War*:

> *"Prime Minister to Secretary of State*
> *for War, CIGS, and General Ismay.*

"It is essential that the French should share in such evacuations from Dunkirk as may be possible. Nor must they be dependent only upon their own shipping resources. Arrangements must be concerted at once with the French Missions in this country, or, if necessary, with the French Government, so that no reproaches, or as few as possible, may arise. It might perhaps be well if we evacuated the two

French divisions from Dunkirk, and replaced them *pro tem* with our own troops, thus simplifying the command. But let me have the best proposals possible, and advise me whether there is any action I should take."

*

"*Prime Minister to General Spears (Paris)*
'*Following for Reynaud, for communication*
'*to Weygand and Georges:*

"We have evacuated nearly 50,000 from Dunkirk and beaches, and hope another 30,000 tonight. Front may be beaten in at any time or piers, beaches, and shipping rendered unusable by air attack, and also by artillery fire from the south-west. No one can tell how long present good flow will last, or how much we can save for future. We wish French troops to share in evacuation to fullest possible extent, and Admiralty have been instructed to aid French Marine as required. We do not know how many will be forced to capitulate, but we must share this loss together as best we can, and, above all, bear it without reproaches arising from inevitable confusion, stresses, and strains.

"As soon as we have reorganised our evacuated troops, and prepared forces necessary to safeguard our life against threatened and perhaps imminent invasion, we shall build up a new B.E.F. from St. Nazaire. I am bringing Regulars from India and Palestine; Australians and Canadians are arriving soon. At present we are removing equipment south of Amiens beyond what is needed for five divisions. But this is only to get into order and meet impending shock, and we shall shortly send you new scheme for reinforcement of our troops in France. I send this in all comradeship. Do not hesitate to speak frankly to me."

*

29

The German squeeze on the trapped Allied forces near the coast extended over an area from the Lys to Gravelines on one side of Dunkirk and to Nieuport on the other side, with a group cut off and encircled at Calais; then the main squeeze was compressed down to about five miles from the port and a few miles on either side of the coast. The Germans announced that the British army, compressed into the territory around Dunkirk, "is going to its destruction before our concentric attack." On 24th May, Hitler halted the German armoured forces and gave Air Marshal Hermann Goering the simple task – he thought – of hammering with his fighters and bombers all the thousands of troops to death or surrender: a serious mistake for Adolf.

On 26th May, the Admiralty signalled to Admiral Ramsay at Dover that Operation Dynamo was to commence. Dover was the main base for the operation and had already suffered heavy bombing attacks; there were ships and boats tied up in threes along the piers; and there were eight berths for cross-Channel steamers. In the coming operation to rescue troops from France, Allied ships and crafts of all types would number some 1,000 of which some 250 would be sunk and scores damaged. There were cruisers, destroyers, smaller warships, trawlers and drifters, MT and A-S boats, Dutch *Schuits*, yachts, pleasure boats, ferries and other assorted craft: all of them came under the strafing or bombardment thrown at them by the Luftwaffe. The *Mona Queen* was one of the civilian boats, an Isle of Man packet, whose master, Captain Duggan took her into the rescue. He later reported:

"Shells were flying all around us. The first salvo went over us. I thought the next salvo would hit us, but fortunately it dropped short, right under our stern. The ship was riddled with shrapnel, mostly all on the boat and promenade decks. Then we were attacked from the air. A Junkers bomber made a power dive towards us and dropped five bombs, but he was off the mark too, I should say about 150 feet from us. All this while we were still being shelled, although we were getting out of range. The Junkers that bombed us was shot down and crashed into the water just ahead of us (no survivors). Then another Junkers attacked us, but before he reached us he was brought down in flames. Then the tension eased a little.

"Owing to the bombardment, I could see that the nerves of some of my men were badly shaken. I did not feel too well myself, but I mustered the crew and told them that Dunkirk was being bombed and was on fire. On being asked if they would volunteer to go in they did so to a man and I am glad to say we took off as many as *Mona Queen* could carry."

Goering was doing his best to bring added glory to his air forces which had previously won the fight to dominate France in the air. The air fighting now was above the clouds and out of sight of the soldiers and ships who were seeing too many black crosses and not enough roundels. Dunkirk certainly was ablaze, from oil tanks and warehouses near the wharves to the office buildings and rows of residential houses; in the harbour the toll of wrecked ships added to the hazards of moving in to pick up men, so ships were ordered to spread along the beaches from where small boats could come in, either to carry them home or transfer them to larger vessels. Tying up at Dunkirk during an air attack was described by the chief officer of a Channel ferry, *Queen of the Channel*:

"Our guns with others were in action. We landed a man on the pier to hang on to our ropes. About 8 p.m. Lieutenant-Commander Williams, RN, came on board and told the captain to proceed out of the harbour, lower his boats and get the men on board from the beach. We got to the anchorage ... When I was about to lower the fourth boat we received the information that there were a number of troops arriving at the pier. With the remainder of the crew we still had on board we proceeded alongside the pier.

We got about 600 men on board. They were arriving in batches. About 11 p.m. we were told there were no more men in the vicinity, so we cut our mooring ropes. On hearing more men running along the pier we got the ship alongside the pier again and got about 80 more men on board. During our stay alongside the pier we had four air raids. While we were leaving the pier the enemy dropped illuminated parachutes which lit up the whole sea front. Our Captain backed the vessel up the harbour under the smoke screen made available to us from the burning town of Dunkirk.

"We then proceeded to try and pick up our boats and crew . . ."

*

Admiral Darlan sent a telegram to Admiral Abrial, who was supervising the French side of the assistance at Dunkirk, ordering him to take note of these measures:

"A bridgehead shall be held round Dunkirk with the divisions under your command and those under British command. As soon as you are convinced that no troops outside the bridgehead can make their way to the points of embarkation the troops holding the bridgehead shall withdraw and embark, the British forces embarking first."

The French army leaders were surprised to learn that the Dunkirk evacuation had started and was on such a large scale. It was explained to them that there were British administrative units sent away first and before fighting troops were brought back from the front. On a visit to Paris, Churchill informed the French that he thought it would be a miracle if, as well as holding the Germans off the beachhead, 200,000 able-bodied troops might be got away. He also said that British troops would form the rearguard and that the French at Dunkirk would be evacuated on equal terms with British troops.

French destroyers and submarine chasers had shot up hundreds of Germans and their equipment on the Dutch coast, and helped bring out trapped French troops. The German advance there was so rapid that Commander Fournière, giving orders to men on the wharf at Walcheren to take his lines, suddenly realised, when he was shot through both cheeks, that he was calling out to Germans to help him tie up the *Bouclier*.

The French 2nd Destroyer Flotilla under the command of Captain Yves Urvoy de Porzamparc, flying his flag in *Cyclone*, raced to Boulogne to fire all their ammunition at German tanks, guns and troops attacking the port. The German tank commander Guderian called up Luftwaffe bombers and the destroyer *Orage* was set on fire and abandoned. While the French destroyers raced to Cherbourg for more ammunition a squadron of British destroyers went into Boulogne to rescue over 4,000 British troops, literally from under the guns of the Germans. When the enemy moved into the town a French petty officer shot a German in the act of hoisting a swastika flag over a building. That was primarily a French battle around Boulogne; at Calais it was more a British battle against the enemy's land and air forces. The destroyer *Chacal* was hit by two aerial bombs and sank, taking with her many of the crew although she was near a jetty.

On 28th May, the French Navy became more heavily involved in the evacuation. Rear-Admiral Marcel Landriau took command of the "Pas-de-Calais Flotilla" – some 250 vessels ranging from two large destroyers and seven fleet destroyers down to sloops and patrol vessels; his command ship was the sloop *Savorgnan de Brazza* in which he sailed to join Admiral Ramsay in Dover Castle. From Brest the old battleships *Courbet* and *Paris* sailed to Cherbourg to bring their anti-aircraft batteries into action against constant black-crossed targets diving and turning over the town and port; when they arrived the air attacks had lifted. The

French ships – men-o'-war and merchantmen – ferried as many as their holds and decks could carry. The *Bourrasque* went down with 1,200 men on board, *Siroco* took 500 men to Dover and on the next day was hit by two torpedoes fired from an E-boat and finished off by bombs dropped from Stukas. The *Mistral* had her bridge wrecked and was forced to limp to Dover without passengers.

Men were wading into the sea and sometimes just stood there waiting for the Navy to do the rest. And the Allied Navy accomplished miracles, as did the RAF fighters to whom the Prime Minister accorded a victory, won in a great trial of strength between the two air forces. At the time, however, the men on the ground and in the sea saw only the bombers and strafing fighters that escaped the constant patrols and attacks by RAF spitfires, Hurricanes and other fighters. Some fighter pilots made so many sorties without rest they were falling asleep in the cockpits of their fighters while waiting to be refuelled.

The failure of Goering's Luftwaffe to prevent the escape of a large, trapped army dismayed the German generals who could have been much more successful with their tanks, guns and infantry. General Halder later said with some bitterness:

"Goering, who knew his Fuehrer well, took advantage of his anxiety. He offered to fight the great battlement of encirclement alone with his Luftwaffe, thus eliminating the risk of having to use the valuable Panzer formations. He wanted to secure for his air force, after the surprisingly smooth operations of the army up to then, the decisive final act in the great battle, and thus gain the glory of success before the whole world." Another German officer said after the war that Goering "kept his finger where he kept his suicide pill."

At Calais there were a cruiser and several destroyers of the Royal Navy standing by while Brigadier C. N. Nicholson's infantry and a collection of French soldiers and sailors fought on instead of evacuating as planned: unfortunately a newly arrived infantry brigade and armoured regiment had destroyed their tanks and trucks in readiness to leave. French coastal guns supported the British ships firing over the town at advancing enemy columns as they fought a bitter struggle with the defenders.

At Dunkirk the evacuation continued with many instances of courage and inventiveness displayed under the trying conditions. An old paddle-ship, the minesweeper *Oriole*, was without boats to bring in men from the shore so her captain drove her onto the beach, forming a pier over which men scrambled to ships coming alongside her stern. One of her officers recorded the operation:

"Everybody went aft to raise the bows as much as possible, and we went lickety-split for the shore and kept her full ahead until we jarred and came to a full stop. As we went in we dropped two 7-cwt. anchors from the stern, to kedge off with. The men waded and swam out and many of them had to be hauled over the rails. The snag was that when a rope was thrown to a man, about six grabbed it and just hung on looking up blankly with the water breaking over their shoulders, and it was a hell of a job getting any of them to let go so that the rest could be pulled overboard." German pilots were amazed to see the old paddle-steamer heading back to England.

On the beach, huge sand-puffs were continually being thrown in the air as bombs dropped among the waiting, tired, hungry and thirsty troops, their confidence restored a little by the remarkably small number of casualties caused by the bombs and the non-stop efforts of the indefatigable sailors. The minesweeper *Emile Deschamps* went down with about 400 men when she hit a mine near the English coast. One of those rescued was Lieutenant de Vaux who had previously been sunk in the destroyer *Jaguar*, another was Captain Cras who was repatriated to France where he was to serve in the Vichy Navy; de Vaux joined the Free

French Naval Forces, and when they both met in Paris after the liberation they greeted each other with "You Dirty Vichyite" and "You dirty Gaullist", then celebrated their reunion in a bar.

One of the last strange sights of the final scene was reported by Mr. R. B. Brett of the *Medway Queen*: "I sighted a *causeway* about eight feet wide heading out into the water! To my surprise, I found it to be a perfectly ordered straight column of men about six abreast, standing as if on parade. When I reached them a sergeant stepped up to me and said, 'Yes sir, sixty men, sir?' He then walked along the column, which remained in perfect formation and detailed the required number to follow me." This was in answer to Brett's call for sixty men to wade out to the boat.

In the great crisis French and British soldiers and sailors proved the existence of a harmonious *entente* between them, and there was no doubt then that the common purpose of the two navies was to fight the Germans to the bitter end.

It was more than the miracle of saving 200,000; the total was 338,226 men including some 123,000 French, two-thirds of whom were brought out by the Royal Navy. When the last evacuees arrived in England, King George VI sent a telegram to the President of the French Republic expressing gratitude and admiration for the part played by the French Armed Forces and sympathy for France's losses.

*

Unfortunately, the end was near for France, and among her leaders there was already bitterness stirring in their hearts. Weygand insisted that General Gort had disobeyed his orders by retreating towards the sea; Darlan accused the British of withdrawing anti-aircraft batteries and search-lights from Le Havre; and the French Air Force General Vuillemin demanded twenty RAF fighter squadrons – some of which Churchill wanted to send and was restrained by

Air Marshal Dowding, who foresaw that Britain would need every fighter she had in the near future, and lost popularity with Churchill for saying so. Anyway, there was little chance of moving a British force, now without the bulk of its equipment, to another part of the French coast, and why were the troops of the Maginot Line left with their useless purpose and facing the wrong way?

France's destiny for the immediate future was obvious: Britain's on the other hand was indefinite and very dangerous. More than 68,000 men of the Expeditionary Force had been killed, wounded or taken prisoner. Material losses included 2,400 guns, 85,000 vehicles and motor cycles, and over half a million tons of stores and equipment. In the evacuation alone Britain had lost six destroyers and nineteen damaged as well as a high proportion of the other two hundred-odd vessels lost. And the RAF was weakened, not only by the loss of aircraft and skilled pilots – there were many damaged fighters which would take a long time to repair, and time, as Dowding knew, was short.

Chapter 4

ARMISTICE

June 13: The Prime Minister flew to Tours to meet M. Reynaud who was now France's Premier. Churchill was informed that Weygand had reported the French armies exhausted and felt it was necessary to ask for an armistice. M. Reynaud said that his countrymen had suffered as much as they could bear and had done their best as a loyal ally. He now asked whether Great Britain would release France from the pledge she had made not to make a separate peace.

Churchill replied that Britain was determined to fight on and was not in a position to release France from her obligation. "Whatever happened," he added, "we would level no reproaches or recriminations" at France; but that was a different matter from consenting to release her from her pledge.

There were still four British divisions fighting in France to which Churchill promised first of all the Canadian division which was on its way, and in the spring twenty-five British divisions – if France could arm them, for Britain was sorely depleted of equipment and armaments. There was no hope left for a miracle and Weygand said, "It was I who read the armistice terms to the Germans twenty years ago. You can imagine how I feel now!"

Churchill also spoke to Darlan, posing a question when he said, "Darlan, you must never let them get the French Fleet." The Admiral replied, "There can be no question of that. It would be contrary to our naval traditions and to our honour." The Prime Minister left Lyon a few days before the Germans who occupied all that part of France they had previously decided they wanted by the end of June.

The fate of the French Navy was now very much on the Prime Minister's mind and the course of history would have changed to Britain's benefit had he trusted Darlan or known that the little Admiral's intention was honest and inflexible – up to a point of who would win the final battle.

Two weeks before the Prime Minister's last visit to France for some years to come, Darlan had issued his secret order: "In the event of a military situation leading to an Armistice which might include a German demand for the surrender of the Fleet, I have no intention of carrying out this order. It may be necessary for the following orders to be given, preparations for which should be made by you in advance and put into effect at the right moment." Predicting that the Italians would enter the war, he issued to his Assistant Chief of Staff a list of possible action:

"If Italy is in the war against us and if she is not a party to the armistice, every available warship should undertake a fight to the death against the Italian Fleet and ports.

"Those ships which are forced to retire from the fight should take refuge in the most accessible British port where they should be ready either to sink themselves or fight with the British.

"If Italy is not in the war, or if she is a party to the armistice, every warship, all naval aircraft and personnel, every naval auxiliary and every seaworthy vessel should concentrate in the nearest British port.

"Every ship (in the West Atlantic) able to cross the Ocean under her own power, by fuelling at sea or by being towed, should endeavour to concentrate at Halifax in Canada.

"Vessels are not to obey an order to return to France or to a port under enemy jurisdiction unless an order is headed – 'In the name of Xavier-François.' "

There was no chance of the Italians grabbing any part of the Fleet, according to those definite orders, but what about the Germans? Already there were French politicians preparing to welcome their old enemy, partly because they admired fascism or because they feared communism. Meanwhile, Churchill was thinking of means to encourage the French to stick by their pledge.

June 16: At 10 Downing Street on that afternoon's meeting of the War Cabinet, the Prime Minister brought up a discussion on a proposal for an indissoluble union of the British and French peoples. He had seen General de Gaulle who had impressed on him that some very dramatic move was essential to give M. Reynaud the support he needed to keep his Government in the war.

At 3.55 p.m. news was received in the Cabinet room: that the French Council of Ministers would meet to decide whether further resistance was possible; that General de Gaulle had been informed by M. Reynaud on the telephone that if a favourable answer on the proposal of unity was received by 5 p.m., M. Reynaud felt that he would be able to hold the position.

The War Cabinet approved the draft Proclamation of an *Anglo-French Union* which declared that France and Great Britain shall no longer be two nations, but one Franco-British Union, *providing a constitution for joint defence and economic policies, and giving all citizens equal right in both countries.* There would be a single War Cabinet governing from wherever it could, and the two Parliaments would be formally associated.

Whether such a union would have survived the post-war political complexities of both countries is open to conjecture. It was a sound political move at the time and when Britain joins France in the European Common Market she will be achieving something Churchill and de Gaulle proposed in 1940.

June 17: A telegram was received from the British Ambassador where he was in touch with the new French Government formed under Marshal Pétain. Admiral Darlan was named as Minister of the Navy, and in another telegram Sir Ronald Campbell quoted the Admiral as saying, "So long as I can issue the orders to it (the French Fleet) you have nothing to fear." At noon Marshal Pétain broadcast that he had asked the enemy to end hostilities, and the following day the British hoped to find a French fleet sailing towards her ports.

June 18: The War Cabinet was informed that Admiral Darlan had informed the First Lord and Chief of Naval Staff that it was his intention to continue the fight, with the French Naval Forces at his disposal, whatever orders he might receive, and the French Admiral in Command at Cherbourg had stated his intention, if need be, of sailing with the ships under his command to England.

There was still hope, despite the evil portent of the discovery of an unexploded time-bomb found in a hold of the SS *City of Sydney* when being unloaded at Mauritius.

June 19: Reports were received of the French Navy going into action against the Italians, bombarding their coast and sinking two of their submarines. The First Lord of the Admiralty reported that he had been favourably impressed with Admiral Darlan who was confident that the French Fleet would obey him. "He seemed," said the First Lord, "determined to ensure that the French ships did not fall into the hands of the Germans. The battleship *Richelieu* was already on her way to Dakar and the *Jean Bart* would be sunk if she could not be towed to England." Demolition of oil stocks and harbour facilities would be carried out and ships unable to put to sea would be destroyed.

Admiral Darlan was reportedly calm and determined, and during the conversation (which took place at Bordeaux) steadfastly maintained that in no circumstances would the French Fleet be surrendered. It would not be possible at present, however, to send the Fleet to British ports. French troops were still fighting, he said, and in the circumstances the Fleet could not desert the country but must remain in French waters until France surrendered. (That was odd, to say the least, for why shouldn't some units go

41

to British ports unless Darlan knew that the Germans would insist that they didn't?)

Resistance had not yet ceased, Darlan continued, and Marshal Pétain at no time issued an order to the troops to lay down their arms – "cesser le combat". Statements to this effect were untrue, he said. The *Richelieu* had sailed for Dakar where she would be worked up, a process that could not be satisfactorily carried out at British bases. If it were impossible to tow the *Jean Bart* she would be blown up. He went on to explain that there would be time to get the Fleet away, if necessary, while negotiations were being conducted.

While the British naval chiefs thought enviously of those lovely French destroyers, so too did the Germans, and Darlan was planning to keep them for his own clique of friends to use as a bargaining weapon and an insurance. If the German terms were too harsh, Britain may get the ships; if not too harsh then they would still be in French hands, even if "France" meant French North Africa. Perhaps Britain too might be conquered by the awesome *Boches* . . .

*

Italy declared war on Britain and France the day Norway capitulated – 10th June. The pressures mounting against the resources of the Royal Navy were reflected in Britain's hardening attitude to France; there was a strong possibility of a German invasion across the Channel, a threat which was all the more dangerous because of Britain's shortage of arms – there were more than enough troops at home but in the Middle East the garrisons were maintained by small numbers, compared with the size of the Italian forces west of Egypt and in Somaliland. Fortunately, when the time came to challenge the Italian invasion from Libya into Egypt, the enemy proved to be as hopeless as in the

First War and they were captured in tens of thousands.

The Italians crept in for the spoils too late to do battle with their battleships and cruisers against the French. The first outstanding loss by the enemy was when the Australian cruiser *Sydney* sank the cruiser *Bartolomeo Colleoni*. The British Mediterranean Fleet, commanded by Admiral Cunningham whose flag was worn by the battleship *Warspite*, comprised three other battleships – *Ramilles*, *Royal Sovereign* and *Malaya* – nine cruisers including *Sydney*, the aircraft carrier *Eagle*, the monitor *Terror*, twenty-six destroyers – four of which were detached to the East Indian Station – twelve submarines and various auxiliary vessels.

The combined British and French fleets in the Mediterranean were about equal with the Italians in cruiser strength, had more capital ships and were about one third weaker in destroyers and submarines. With the French ships taken out, Mussolini could be excused for referring to the Sea as *Mare Nostrum*. Fortunately for Britain, the battle efficiency of the Italians was weak and their ships, though fast, lacked adequate protective armour, too much space was devoted to luxurious officers' quarters and there was a lack of engineering and scientific development. The gulf between the officers' and mens' quarters was also striking in their desert establishments where the Allied armies found perfume, nude pin-ups and rosary beads on tables littered with cognac and wine bottles in officers' quarters, while in the men's dugouts were rosary beads, fleas and filth. On Italian destroyers and corvettes the bridges were covered or built-in for protection against the elements; not at all, thought the British, conducive to rugged efficiency. Morale was weakened by the strutting arrogance of officers and the sketchy training given to recruits. Nevertheless, the Italian Navy could prove to be very dangerous.

*

43

After 17th June there was no longer any co-ordinated French defence against the Germans except on the Loire sector and it was only a matter of waiting for the armistice. The Reynaud Cabinet fell the previous night to be replaced by a Pétain government whose first action was to ask the Germans for an armistice. Another Battle of the Somme was the beginning of the end; a pincer movement was made towards Paris which had been declared an "open city" and was entered by Germans on the 14th. During these disasters Marshal Pétain was already drawing up his list of what some may call "collaborators". The Germans and Italians were asked for their armistice terms through the intermediary of Madrid and the Vatican.

The Germans were also prepared, the first draft of an armistice having been drawn up by General Keitel, providing for the total occupation of France. Then Hitler gave fresh instructions, saying that France "had to be cut off from Britain and to do this she must obtain terms appearing to make up for this. Since the Pétain government appeared to be favourably disposed, it had to be given a 'golden bridge'; otherwise there would still be a risk of the French government escaping to North Africa with its fleet and some of its aircraft, to continue the war there." Very cunning indeed. "This," continued der Fuehrer, "would strengthen Britain's position and stir up the war in the Mediterranean, where Italy was in an isolated position." There was strong opposition from the hungry Italians when Hitler defined his demands, the bait for the desperate French being their Fleet:

"The French government must survive as a sovereign power. Only in this way can we be certain that the French colonial empire will not go over to Britain.

"Thus a total occupation of metropolitan France is inadvisable. The French government must retain a sphere of sovereignty.

"The French army will be taken to the free zone and de-

mobilised there. The preservation of some units in a free zone must be permitted in order to maintain order. The fleet must be neutralised. Under no circumstances must we demand its hand-over, otherwise it would withdraw overseas to Britain.

"The territorial demands are a matter for the peace settlement, which cannot be discussed at present.

"No demand concerning the empire will be formulated for the moment. This would only drive the colonies to Britain. Moreover, in case of refusal, we could not put these demands into effect by force at present."

It is intriguing to think of how many *French* ideas were incorporated into these ingredients of future breaks with Britain; it is doubtful if Hitler then thought Britain might use force against the French Fleet and so make enemies among her former allies. Also, Hitler then did not know how determined Britain was to fight back, even to the extent of risking a break in the battle-tried spirit of *entente*.

Colonel Bohme, one of Keitel's staff officers, later wrote that the Fleet was the main question: it could represent a great increase in power to Britain, and its loss would represent a *great* loss. Suddenly the French Fleet, which could be a colossal danger if it were allowed to go into action, was to be cut off from its own country and left without a friend; it was virtually outlawed.

The Germans were ready to announce terms for a cessation of hostilities on 19th June; they had advance troops entering Bordeaux from where Pétain and his government had fled to Perpignan to avoid capture, although by now capture and check-mate were unnecessary for the game was over. They had prepared to fly to North Africa when Laval led a delegation of parliamentarians to meet him and discuss the military situation; the flight was cancelled and Pétain declared that he favoured an early peace because of "Britain's desperate situation." Two days later delegates met the Germans in the Sedan railway carriage which had

45

been preserved as a memorial to the scene of the 1918 Armistice. The negotiations dragged on for days. "We have to keep the French holding on and extract all we can in the meantime," noted diarist Goebbels.

On 25th June it was all over. "Honour is saved!" announced Pétain over the radio, "A new order is beginning." A couple of weeks later he adopted the royal "we" when he announced that the Republic was abolished, parliament dismissed and he assumed functions of Head of the French State. In future, newly minted coins would not be stamped with "République Française" and "Liberté, Égalité and Fraternité", instead they would be stamped with "Etat Francais" and the heavily Germanic "Travail Famille Patrie". Much of the "Travail" would be done by forced French labour in Germany, and in the French underground the word for Resistance was Travail. The Atlantic seaboard was gone from the new State and the centre of government was at the spa town of Vichy, twenty-five miles from road points where German soldiers erected barriers. Colonel Adolph Goutard, who fought in the Italian campaign and the liberation of France, wrote a reasonable summation of why France accepted the terms:

"The main error had been that our highest leaders were convinced that a rapid German victory was pre-ordained. France, the leading military power on the Continent, had therefore been defeated. 'Britain,' General Weygand repeated incessantly in his vivid language, was to have her 'neck wrung like a chicken,' while Russia, he maintained, was Germany's 'ally'." And America refused to intervene.

"What – in their eyes – could stop Hitler remodelling Europe as he liked? Was it not better to get him to formulate his peace terms before he had defeated Britain, his last enemy – because his terms would doubtless be worse when he was in the rapture of a total victory? Moreover, would not Hitler be more indulgent to a France with an authoritarian regime like those of Germany and Italy, and *after* it had entered into the 'new European order' deliberately?

"It was therefore not a question of treason, against either France or the Allied cause. The men asking Hitler for peace were French patriots who on the contrary wished to save their country from total destruction, so that it could survive and gradually make its mark in the new Europe which was to arise. As for the Allied cause, nobody could betray it for it was lost! Thus it was all simply a question of errors in calculation, errors which President Lebrun defined perfectly as follows: 'Two errors were committed: there was a conviction of German victory, and Marshal Pétain believed that his prestige would suffice to protect the country and defend it.'

"A misapprehension of the possibility of a German victory in a war which was destined to become worldwide, plus a deplorable ignorance of the nature of Hitler's meglomania, was therefore responsible for the tragedy."

In all fairness, it is understandable that when such reasoning was spread among the people it would be readily acceptable as an honest summation of the situation. However, the war was still in progress and under those conditions there could be no "re-birth of France" – and there were other ideas, voiced loudly and strongly and persuasively by Churchill and de Gaulle in the most reliable source of information – the BBC – to which all thinking men listened; if there was an inclination to passiveness and complacency it evaporated as the war went on, and on, and on.

*

In accordance with arrangements made with the British Admiralty by Admiral Odend'hal, the *Richelieu* which was undergoing sea trials at Brest, and the *Jean Bart* (named after the 17th century admiral who, with only five frigates kept more than 50 British and Dutch warships at sea), these two battleships, one without an engine-test and the

47

other with uncompleted turrets, were to be towed to England in case, Darlan said, "we should be surprised by the rapidity of events." That was the intention on 15th June. The following day the panzers were swinging in to move towards Brest and Cherbourg, and Rommel, in command of this armoured force, ran into a strong defence controlled by Admiral Abrial; the German was delayed long enough for British troops to be evacuated as well as all the French ships in Cherbourg. An unlaunched submarine was blown up. Abrial, Le Bigot and the garrison were taken prisoner.

At Brest, Admiral de Laborde, C-in-C West, was instructed to load some 1,000 tons of gold into his auxiliary cruisers in port and carry it out to Dakar; he had gold, British troops, French troops and Germans converging towards his port when a captured French general telephoned through, on an uncut line, that there were no French troops left in front of Brest. He estimated that he had ten hours in which to get 159 ships out of the harbour as well as wreck the installations and burn the fuel. Later, when being tried by the French for scuttling the fleet at Toulon, he was asked why he had not answered de Gaulle's broadcast call to arms on the 18th, and he replied that he "had other things to do besides listening to the British Broadcasting Corporation." Of the 83 warships in port, 74 got away and nine were destroyed; one merchantman was scuttled, one was lost to enemy action and the rest escaped, taking with them General Bethouart's brigade recently returned from the Narvik campaign.

Winston Churchill, historian, wrote that "not one French warship moved in order to place itself out of reach of the German troops," a statement quite incorrect, as the Fleet's historians, Auphan and Mordal point out. Perhaps Churchill meant that not one of the ships moved *to England* to place itself out of reach.

The old *Paris* slipped out of drydock and *Richelieu* sailed majestically away with all the French Naval Academy's midshipmen aboard; the huge *Surcouf* had her driving innards apart and spread about the concrete-topped pen, waiting for new diesels and accumulators, and when she was ordered away her crew shoved the parts back as quickly as they could and she went out on her electric motors with one diving rudder jammed hard over.

The *Jean Bart* was at Saint-Nazaire where British transports were helping to evacuate 40,000 British and 2,500 Polish troops, the bulk of whom were one day to conquer more than that number of Germans. The escape of the battleship was spectacular, as Auphan and Mordal describe so well in *The French Navy in World War II*:

"The uncompleted ship, with workmen's scaffolds still covering the decks, was afloat in an open basin separated from the ship channel by an earthen dike. This dike had to be dredged out before the ship could reach open water.

"In normal years there would have been ample time to complete the dredging before the ship's scheduled departure in October. But without waiting for orders the commanding officer had begun dredging on May 25, when the military situation had begun to turn worse. From then on it was a race against time.

"But even with the dike dredged away, it would be necessary to get the ship out on the high tides between June 18 and 22, or else wait weeks for the next ones. And there could be no waiting. The high tide of the night of June 18 was selected for the departure. But within that short time it would be possible to dredge only to a depth of 8.1 metres, which meant that the ship would have to go out almost completely stripped – no water, no provisions, no fuel oil, and only one of her 380mm turrets in place. Also, there would be no time to dredge the channel any wider than 50 metres; the *Jean Bart* herself was 35 metres wide. By extraordinary exertions the dredging was completed by 2 o'clock on the morning of the 19th.

"One boiler in the fireroom had been ready since June

11, but only two of the four propellers were in place. The turbine drives for these two propellers had been hurriedly installed, but the engines had not yet been turned over under their own power. Not a gun aboard was in condition to fire, so a few anti-aircraft machine-guns, a few 37mm guns, and two 90mm twin mounts were hurriedly swung aboard and bolted down.

"Already, as it was learned, the Germans were at Rennes; they would reach Saint-Nazaire the next day. If the *Jean Bart* did not leave that very night, there would be nothing left to do but blow her up.

"At 0330, the time of high tide, the operation began. There was no power on the main engines, or on the rudder, or the windlass, or the aft winches. Everything had to be done by hand – with capstan bars aboard and pushing tugs outboard. The ship managed to get clear of the basin without too much difficulty, but in the darkness she missed a buoy in the too narrow channel and ran aground. It took six tugs to pull her off again. Then at 0440, just as the *Jean Bart* was clearing the entrance to the Loire, the Luftwaffe appeared. The ship sustained but one hit, and that caused only minor damage. Then after the German attack was over, the French fighter planes, which had been scheduled to give air cover, belatedly arrived – and were warmly greeted by the *Jean Bart*'s gunners. Luckily only one Morane fighter was hit, and no lives were lost.

"Then, little by little everything straightened out. Luck was with the ship. The main engines began to turn over; there was steam for the auxiliaries, and electric power for the steering; the oil tankers were on time at the refuelling rendezvous; and two German submarines, which had been lying in wait, never made contact.

"The *Jean Bart* was saved. Even though she had no steering compass, she could follow the destroyer *Hardi*, on which Admiral de Laborde had hoisted his flag. At 1700 on June 22, the *Jean Bart* steamed into Casablanca harbour, in French Morocco, having made the whole trip at an average speed of 21 knots." The battleship was commanded by Captain Pierre Ronarc'h.

Elsewhere there was a general exodus from French ports and British destroyers managed to head some of them to England. The British Admiralty approved of a bribe of one hundred pounds to be paid by a British liaison officer at Bordeaux to the captain of the freighter *Fort Medine*. The bribe was to be paid, if necessary, to get the ship to England since it carried the archives of the Gnome and Rhone aircraft engine factory. The freighter went to England. Other merchant ships failed to go anywhere because of low morale among sailors who knew that their war was lost and had no desire to risk their necks unnecessarily. Perhaps some were influenced by Russian propaganda which was at that time very anti-British.

Like the Italians, the Russians had made their grab of the spoils: they took Lithuania and Estonia and threatened Romania with violence unless she handed over a couple of provinces. The Italians made a highly publicised attack across the border, from the mountains down to the sea near Nice, and were firmly held by French forces inferior in strength and threatened at the rear by German armoured units. With a little more time the French troops would have won themselves quite a large area of northern Italy.

One of the British destroyers sniffing at French ships pulling away from their ports was HMS *Vanquisher* with Vice-Admiral Hallett on board. He was there to ensure that *Jean Bart* got away – to anywhere – and if not he was to go into Saint-Nazaire and sink the battleship.

*

A few days before the surrender, Churchill was predicting in a letter to Roosevelt that the French Fleet would be used as bait on one side and as a bargaining weapon on the other.

"Have you considered," he asked, "what offers Hitler may choose to make to France? He may say: 'Surrender the Fleet intact and I will leave you Alsace-Lorraine,' or alternatively: 'If you do not give me your ships I will destroy your towns.'"

The actual clauses concerning the Fleet were written in Articles 8 and 9 of the Franco-German armistice convention:

Article 8. The French war fleet, with the exception of that part permitted to the French Government for the protection of French interests in its colonial empire, is to be assembled in ports to be specified and disarmed under German or Italian control. The choice of these ports will be determined by the peacetime stations of the ships. The German Government solemnly declares to the French Government that it does not intend to use for its own purposes in the war the French Fleet which is in ports under German control, with the exception of those units needed for coastal patrol and for minesweeping. Furthermore, it solemnly and expressly declares that it has no intention of raising any claim to the French war fleet at the time of the conclusion of peace, With the exception of that part of the French war fleet, still to be determined, which is to represent French interests in the colonial empire, all war vessels which are outside French territorial waters are to be recalled to France.

Article 9. The French High Command is to provide the German High Command with detailed information about all mines laid by France, as well as all harbour and coastal barriers and installations of defence and protection. The clearing of minefields is to be carried out by French forces to the extent required by the German High Command.

Promises, promises, by the biggest liars in the world's diplomatic corps. However, until the lies were revealed, the Fleet would at least be in French hands and it was inconceivable that their guns would ever be aimed at British ships and fired on German orders. And what, wondered the British Cabinet members when a copy of the Articles was shown them, was meant by "disarmed under German control". The word "contrôle", as used in the French translation of the Article 8, means surveying, mustering, listing and registering. To the British, the word "control" meant, or inferred, a power to direct. Anyway, the War Cabinet simply did not trust the Germans, who had broken their word so often: hadn't the war itself begun because of broken German pledges? And with a break in the direct communications between the old allies a mistrust of the French was permeating the discussions of the British leaders.

The distrust spread to both sides, increased among the French by Britain's new friend, de Gaulle, when he made his broadcast speech over the BBC radio. In denouncing the new French government he was denouncing Darlan as a member of the "makeshift" team. The *honneur* of French officers was under attack, even though Darlan and his Admirals in the pecking order had promised to scuttle the Fleet if there was ever a danger of it falling into Axis hands. Distrust increased in Britain when it was known that Pierre Laval was a member of the new French government, having been previously excluded because he was anti-British.

A French counter-proposal to Article 8 might have eased the tension at Downing Street had the news reached there: Darlan's Chief of Staff, Admiral Le Luc, told the Germans that no French warships would be returning to their old ports if those ports were on the Atlantic coast – now completely occupied by Germans – and he proposed that the Fleet should be demobilised at Toulon and the North and West African ports. Keitel said that he would accept the proposals in principle without allowing any modification to the draft of the armistice Articles.

The Italians gained very little from their armistice with France, signed on the 24th, two days after the Germans.

British envoys still in France could do no more and prepared to go home. It was too late now to send British
troops to Casablanca and elsewhere to stiffen French
morale; in any case anti-British propaganda in Casablanca
had had some success, judging by the cold reception received by British evacuees from Gibraltar.

French morale was low everywhere, understandably. It
was undoubtedly true, as a French capitaine de corvette
asserted at Falmouth, that there was a strong feeling among
French naval officers in favour of continuing the fighting.
He had spoken contemptuously of French politicians as a
whole, and had said that feeling would run high among his
brother officers if there were any attempts to include French
politicians in the French National Committee in London.
However, the view generally expressed was that, whatever
the sentiments of individual officers, there was very little
hope that the French nation as a whole would continue the
fight.

Chapter 5

THE OUTLAWED NAVY

THE British were now becoming a little more active regarding the French warships and merchant ships; and the French were beginning to complain about the hold-up of French ships in Britain.

While the War Cabinet awaited the outcome of the Franco-German and Franco-Italian armistices, the First Lord of the Admiralty said that the French authorities were becoming apprehensive about Britain's treatment of French shipping. The Cabinet decided that the French had little cause for complaint, in view of the danger to the Allied cause constituted by the large collection of French shipping which had sailed from French Atlantic ports; that the enemy could seize French ships; that it was considered permissible on humanitarian grounds to allow French ships carrying food to sail to French ports not occupied by the enemy. In accordance with Article 14 of the armistice agreement, all French radios were sealed, and carried messages were taking up to two days to reach their recipients in both countries. Darlan's last broadcast message to his ships was a directive to all commanders to sail for America or scuttle their ships if they were in danger of being seized by Germans or Italians.

In Britain, the War Cabinet was meeting three and four times a day, at each meeting the French Fleet was always made a subject of discussion. German air raids were incoming over the forward fighter stations of south-east England while along the coasts a constant alert was maintained as a German invasion loomed.

On 21st June, the following French warships were in

British ports: the battleship *Courbet*, a destroyer, three submarines, three torpedo boats, a patrol vessel and two submarine chasers at Portsmouth; a destroyer, two submarines, three submarine chasers and six tugs and trawlers at Plymouth. French merchant ships were held up at British ports under various irregular pretexts although a few were allowed to proceed to French colonial ports outside the Mediterranean. The cruiser *Emile Bertin* had arrived in Halifax carrying 300 million dollars worth of gold, consigned from the Bank of France to the Bank of Ottawa, but she moved out from Halifax with the gold and, shadowed by the cruiser HMS *Devonshire*, was allowed to set course for Martinique.

The Admiralty sent a telegram to British admirals at Portsmouth and Plymouth to "grant all facilities to French ships for their departure to North Africa", then soon afterwards the orders were countermanded. The same day, the 22nd, the First Lord said that Admiral Odend'hal, who was at Portsmouth, had received orders from Admiral Darlan that the ships in those ports were to sail to Dakar. The War Cabinet decided that it was not desirable to run the risk of upsetting Darlan by making difficulties about French warships leaving the ports. Warships in the Eastern Mediterranean were still in company with the British Mediterranean Fleet.

A later meeting was held that day when it was agreed to again appeal to Darlan in the form of personal messages from the First Lord and the First Sea Lord, with a view to the vital need for obtaining control of the French Navy. An appeal should also be made to Admiral Estava at Oran where he should be contacted by a deputation. It was also decided that the Admiralty should assume responsibility for making sure that the battleships *Richelieu* and *Jean Bart* did not leave the ports of Dakar and Casablanca, and that French warships in British ports remained there.

The growing threat of an invasion weighed heavily on

the minds of the British leaders; they could be committed to throw into a Channel battle every available ship, and if the Germans arrived with seized French ships the outcome may well have been disastrous. In those circumstances the French Fleet was becoming an obsession, and to help prevent the loss of the French ships, de Gaulle was again asked to broadcast to the French people.

Distrust was spreading as old friends and allies thought and planned on diverging lines.

June 24: To the Cabinet the Prime Minister read a message from M. Reynaud which he had just received through the French Ambassador. M. Reynaud pleaded that there should be no recriminations against the present French Government, and attempted to argue that, notwithstanding the terms of the armistice, the British Government would be safeguarded against the enemy obtaining possession of the French Fleet.

It was clear from this message, decided the Prime Minister, that M. Reynaud could be no more relied on than any of the other members of the government who had broken their solemn treaty obligations and were now completely under the thumb of Germany.

Viscount Halifax, the Secretary of State for Foreign Affairs, said that the French Ambassador had expressed to him on the previous day the grave concern which he and M. Léger felt over "our action in supporting General de Gaulle." M. Reynaud was most anxious to do everything possible to keep resistance alive, but insisted we were not going about it the right way ... he was "horrified" by the terms of General de Gaulle's broadcast ...

A planned Naval mission to Oran was deferred until it was possible to find out if the authorities in Algeria and Tunis were prepared to continue resistance.

*

On the afternoon of 30th June, Admiral Sir Tom Phillips, Deputy Chief of Naval Staff, received a copy of a telegraphed message sent from the French Admiralty to Admiral Odend'hal:

"Italian Government authorises the stationing of the Fleet, with half crews, at Toulon and in North Africa. I have firm hopes that it will be likewise with the German Government, whose reply we are now awaiting. Under these conditions all British pretexts for detaining our forces are without foundation, and I beg of you to insist on our men-of-war and merchantmen being released."

The same consent was actually received that day from the Germans but there was apparently no time to send the verification to Odend'hal in Britain. In France, the Germans were insisting on the return of the French warships from Britain, causing a certain amount of anguish and nervousness in the government and much annoyance to Darlan, for whom the situation was intolerable: he was asking his friends and enemies to trust the French Admiralty – the Germans were trusting him to demobilise the Fleet while the British did not trust his intention of "keeping the ships from the enemy at all costs".

The pressures mounted from both sides until, within twenty-four hours, the French Navy received ultimatums from both the British and the Germans. On 3rd July, the Germans demanded that all French ships must return to France, "or the entire armistice would be reconsidered." The day before, a Most Secret message was sent from the British Admiralty to the Commander-in-Chief, Mediterranean:

His Majesty's Government have decided that the course to be adopted is as follows:

(A) French Fleet at Oran and Mers-el-Kebir is to be given four alternatives:

1. To sail their ships to British harbours and continue the fight with us.

2. *To sail their ships with reduced crews to a British port from which the crews could be repatriated whenever desired.*

In the case of the alternatives (1) or (2) being adopted, the ships would be restored to France at the conclusion of the war or full compensation would be paid if they are damaged meanwhile.

If the French Admiralty accepts alternative (2), but insists that ships should not be used by us during the war you may say we accept this condition for as long as Germany and Italy observe the Armistice terms, but we particularly do not wish to raise the point ourselves.

3. *To sail their ships with reduced crews to some French port in the West Indies such as Martinique.*

After arriving at this port they would either be demilitarised to our satisfaction, or, if so desired, be entrusted to United States jurisdiction for the duration of the war. The crews would be repatriated.

4. *To sink their ships.*

(B) Should the French Admiral refuse to accept all of the above alternatives and should he suggest that he should demilitarise his ships to our satisfaction at their present berths, you are authorised to accept this further alternative provided that you are satisfied that the measures taken for demilitarisation can be carried out under your supervision within six hours and would prevent the ships being brought into service for at least one year, even at a fully equipped dockyard port.

(C) If none of the above alternatives is accepted by the French, you are to endeavour to destroy ships in Mers-el-Kebir, but particularly Dunkerque *and* Strasbourg, *using all means at your disposal. Ships at Oran should also be destroyed if this will not entail any considerable loss of civilian life.*

The message went on to advise that French ships should be dealt with not on the open sea but in port, that because of the strong shore defences at Algiers where it would be impossible to avoid the destruction of the town, it was not considered justifiable to carry out a separate operation against that place.

In conclusion, the message stated that these were *final* instructions.

The same day a message was sent from the Admiralty to be forwarded to the French Admiral at Oran, asking him to accept demands to fight on, neutralise his ships or see them sunk within six hours.

France had gone to extreme lengths in its hour of defeat to save its Navy from the enemy and had not only succeeded there but found too that she had a bargaining medium of great value.

Britain, in her hour of greatest danger, was fearful of the enemy gaining the use of extra naval power; she ended what was considered to be a time limit for discussions and made a stubborn resolution to adjust the situation by force.

In simple human terms the situation had all the ingredients required to inspire fear and then a brawl.

It happened on 3rd July, 1940, and was coded Operation Catapult.

*

Preparations had begun in late June for the actions which began first with the ships in English ports. Some eight thousand men, mostly passengers or refugees had been taken from the ships in Portsmouth and Plymouth and taken to a camp at Aintree, near Liverpool, to await transport in British ships to Casablanca. Vessels outside the ports had been brought in on various pretexts and on all ships British liaison officers had been installed; the French were completely lulled into a sense of tranquility, rudely shattered before dawn on the 3rd when every ship had a Royal Navy officer presenting himself on its gangplank.

Ships captains were confronted by officers, armed with

pistols, and in old-style boarding method armed men went on board to guard every hatch and passage; the captains were given a memorandum stating that the ship must be handed over to the boarding officer and all crews were prevented from leaving. Royal Marines and infantry were there with fixed bayonets to act quickly in case of resistance, and against some two thousand of them there was not likely to be any.

Two Lieutenant-Commanders, Sprague and Griffiths, boarded the large submarine *Surcouf* in which the French officers were brought into the wardroom, the commanding officer, Paul Martin, insisting on changing from pyjamas to uniform for the occasion. Sprague read to the officers that they were under arrest and that they and the crew would be taken ashore; later, if they wished to be repatriated to French territory they would be allowed to go, or they could stay in Britain and continue the fight against Germany. Since they had all been sounded out on this before it was not expected that they would sit down to deliberate the choice.

Martin asked Sprague if he might visit the battleship *Paris* to discuss the matter with his Admiral, de Villaine, giving his word that he would return immediately after the interview. Sprague agreed to this request from Martin whom he had met before, and also he agreed not to remove anyone from the boat until Martin returned. As Martin was being led away they all heard a shot fired and dashed down into the submarine. With pistol in hand, Sprague ran towards the wardroom and the *Surcouf*'s gunnery officer, Bouillaut, shot him – wounding him in the head.

Griffiths ran towards Bouillaut and hit him with a pistol shot, wounding him in the shoulder; then Griffiths tripped over Sprague's body and as he went down he was shot in the chest and lay bleeding from the mouth. Griffiths had been shot by the submarine's doctor who then fired his automatic at a Marine sergeant lunging forward with his bayonet; before the Marine died he bayoneted to death another Frenchman. First blood had been drawn in the action to neutralise the French Fleet, and fortunately there were no other mortalities in the British ports.

At Plymouth, the *Mistral* began to go down when the boarding party was announced and the officers collected: sea valves had been opened and several compartments were flooded, and she would have continued to the bottom had not the British officer in charge threatened to have the ship's crews, locked in their compartments, go down with the ship. The valves were turned off and the scuttling avoided.

Elsewhere there was little trouble getting all the officers and crews ashore and to camps which were unpleasant and insanitary; when the French admirals asked that the men be allowed to go back to the ships their request was refused – the British did not wish to risk any further scuttling attempts although the battleships *Paris* and *Courbet* were then of little use.

Efforts of course were strenuously made by British and French Liberation people to recruit officers and men to the continuing fight, but their efforts were little more than useless among the disenchanted French; the majority wanted to be repatriated. At the end of July, 1,100 sailed from Southampton on the French passenger ship *Meknès*, bound for unoccupied France; when night fell, the ship sailed on with all lights burning, indicating that she was a neutral, and at 10 p.m. she was hailed by a German torpedo boat but, because she did not stop, the Germans machine-gunned her and then sank her with a torpedo. Loss of life numbered nearly 400, another tragedy blamed on the British by many Frenchmen. Future repatriations were made in hospital ships whose movements were freely announced to ensure safe conduct to France. Some 30,000 seamen, soldiers and civilians were returned home by the end of the year.

*

Everything really depended on the Royal Navy to save Britain from invasion and semi-starvation. RAF action against ships had been hit and miss, with many more misses; in fact it wasn't until Japan showed off her highly skilled dive-bomber and high-level bomber crews that any combatant could boast a devastating anti-ship air arm. With Britain suddenly severed from her old ally, and by thousands of sea miles from friendly America and faithful Dominions, politicians and newspaper editors, soldiers, airmen and the whole populace thought, if they did not talk, of their dependence on the Royal Navy and, of course, the merchant seamen.

While Britain had lost a strong naval ally that June, Germany gained a naval ally – Italy, with fast, modern ships but not what the Royal Navy considered strong. "We are also told that the Italian Navy is to come out and gain superiority in these waters," announced Churchill in his famous speech, broadcast on 18th June. "If they seriously intend it, I shall say that we shall be delighted to offer Signor Mussolini a free and safeguarded passage through the Straits of Gibraltar in order that he may play the part to which he aspires. There is a general curiosity in the British Fleet to find out whether the Italians are up to the level they were at in the last war or whether they have fallen off."

Referring to a possible invasion the Prime Minister said there would be very great possibilities "that this armada would be intercepted long before it reached the coast, and all the men drowned in the sea or, at the worst, blown to pieces with their equipment while they were trying to land. We also have a great system of minefields, recently strongly reinforced, through which we alone know the channels. If the enemy tries to sweep passages through these minefields, it will be the task of the Navy to destroy the minesweepers and any other forces employed to protect them." The Navy was always uppermost in the leaders' thoughts and now that Italy had, jackal-like, entered the war as France was falling, the Mediterranean commitments must weaken the Home Fleet. The presence of the Italian Fleet made the loss of the French Fleet more galling.

In his 18th June speech Churchill paid tribute to the RAF defenders and concluded with the announcement of the Battle of Britain:

"What General Weygand called the Battle of France is over. I expect that the Battle of Britain is about to begin. Upon this battle depends the survival of Christian civilization. Upon it depends our own British life, and the long continuity of our institutions and our Empire. The whole fury and might of the enemy must very soon be turned on us. Hitler knows that he will have to break us in this island or lose the war. If we can stand up to him, all Europe may be free and the life of the world may move forward into broad, sunlit uplands. But if we fail, then the whole world including the United States, including all that we have known and cared for, will sink into the abyss of a new Dark Age made more sinister, and perhaps more protracted, by the lights of perverted science. Let us therefore brace ourselves to our duties, and so bear ourselves that, if the British Empire and its Commonwealth last for a thousand years, men will still say, 'This was their finest hour.'"

In a thousand years men will doubtless say it was Britain's finest hour; in a thousand years the world will be either one commonwealth or one desolation. In 1940, Churchill was inspiring a nation confused, dazed and partly afraid; there is no doubt that his common sense, realism and determination to resist lifted the spirits and strengthened the morale of the British people. Such a leader in France might have sent the French Fleet to British ports – a part of the French people who could have fought on, as an arm of French power which could have been given then without much more retribution by the Germans. And a strong leader out of France may have influenced a large part of the French Fleet to go to British ports, although the immense obstacle would have been those same qualities of efficiency, alertness and obedience, derived from discipline, that were inherent in the British and German as well as the French Navy; discipline and the pecking-order respect which flowed, strict and obedient, from top to bottom and from ordinary seamen all the way up to the Commander-in-Chief. It was that man, the Commander-in-Chief, Admiral Darlan, whom Churchill hated and against whom he led the hate-cry taken up by the Allies and the Free French.

De Gaulle was no substitute then, in French eyes, for Darlan or Weygand or Pétain – and in times of trouble the French people were more inclined to place their trust in military leaders – the Napoleon syndrome – than in politicians. If there had not been a very active Liberation Committee and a determined de Gaulle in England, the British War Cabinet may have placed more trust and been more understanding in France's delicate and highly dangerous situation regarding not only unoccupied metropolitan France but North Africa as well. And with the French Fleet left demilitarised and neutral, and not antagonised by Britain, the French admirals would have been received back in France at the end of hostilities as men who had dutifully performed their duties, and not, as de Gaulle's government demanded, as suspect traitors to go before tribunals for their lives. In all fairness, history must describe the French admirals as being entirely loyal and honourable, and that the fate of some – particularly Derrien, who ended up being chained in a filthy prison – was a disgrace to French justice.

*

When Admiral S. R. Freemantle wrote his memoirs, *My Naval Career 1880–1928*, he made mention of the attack on Oran:

"In all our investigations [into the possibility of a 'bolt from the blue' attack on the British Fleet] we could find two cases only of such hostilities being undertaken unless preceded either by a time of strained relations or a formal declaration of war. These were our attacks on Denmark [Copenhagen] in 1801 and 1807 respectively . . . both of which, though much criticised at home, were in my opinion fully warranted by the strategical situations obtaining, and the successful execution of which secured the desired results."

The Admiralty, however, did not seek precedent as a reason, although relations were slightly strained, and the orders to carry out the demands to the extent of firing on French ships were not at all popular with the Royal Navy, as was pointed out in the House of Lords after the war:

"Admiral North had visited the French Admiral at Oran and had received an assurance that French ships would not be surrendered to Germany or Italy, and he was not alone in being appalled at the decision to attack these French ships at Oran. Admiral Somerville was ordered to carry out the attack, and he and all of the officers concerned *were horror struck by the decision*. Admiral Somerville intended to protest, but before he could do so, he was informed that the decision was the irrevocable decision of the War Cabinet."

The decision was made after the problem had been presented to the War Cabinet as a strategic one with the imminent enemy assault on Britain as the pressure point. To Churchill, it was also a gesture of defiance, as Cordell Hull, United States Secretary of State, later wrote that after having discussed the incident with Churchill, the Prime Minister had said that since many people throughout the world believed that Britain was about to surrender, he wanted by this action to show that she still meant to fight. At the time, people throughout the world did not know how few ships Britain then had to protect her shores and guard her lifelines. Hitler knew, and he had insisted on the French Navy's neutrality, saying at the time of the armistice that six destroyers could always prevent a U-boat attack on an Allied convoy of merchant ships.

When the catastrophe in France was developing to a final decision regarding her ships, it was necessary for the Admiralty to consider the possibilities of the loss of Allied sea power in the Western Mediterranean. To adjust the situation, a force "H", built around the battlecruiser *Hood* and the aircraft carrier *Ark Royal*, was assembled at Gibraltar under Vice-Admiral Sir James Somerville. Admiral of the Fleet Sir Dudley Pound had foreseen the possibility of the ally going out of the war and also the possibility of the ally's ships being taken over by the enemy. Thus when the ultimatum was issued it was Somerville's unpleasant task to take Force H across to confront the French at their Moroccan base. British sailors hoped that they would not have to be the first to fire on French ships after one hundred and twenty-five years without action between them.

The town of Oran is on a ten-mile wide bay and Mers-el-Kebir was the French naval base about four miles west of the town. The docks, piers and anchorages were protected by a net stretched from Cap Falcon to Point Canastel; there was a coastal battery at Mers-el-Kebir and a string of batteries based along the coast north-east of the town. The action that took place in the Bay and at the naval station is popularly known as the battle of Oran.

Behind the stone breakwater extending a mile into the bay from Fort Mers-el-Kebir were moored Admiral Gensoul's four battleships, *Dunkerque*, *Strasbourg*, *Provence* and *Bretagne*. Their sterns were towards the breakwater and therefore the main forward turrets pointed inland: there were no main aft turrets on *Dunkerque* or *Strasbourg*, the more modern ships. Other warships in Gensoul's squadron were the heavy destroyers *Volta*, *Mogador*, *Tigre*, *Lynx*, *Kersaint* and *Le Terrible*, and the seaplane tender *Commandante Teste*, all assembled at piers or at anchor near the Fort. Anchored and moored near the town was another collection of ships recently arrived from Toulon, a mixed fleet of small ships, from light destroyers and sloops down to patrol vessels. The Royal Navy's main interest was the group at Mers-el-Kebir. At Algiers, some 250 sea miles away to the east, was a squadron of six cruisers.

Two cruisers and eleven destroyers escorted the *Hood, Ark Royal, Valiant* and *Resolution* on their overnight cruise from Gibraltar to the sea in front of Oran. At dawn they hove-to while the aircraft carrier's commander, Captain Holland, transferred to the destroyer *Foxhound* to be carried in to parley with the French. During the night Churchill had cabled the *Hood*, "You are charged with one of the most disagreeable and difficult tasks that a British Admiral has ever been faced with, but we have complete confidence in you and rely on you to carry it out relentlessly." Admiral Somerville thought it worse than disagreeable and no doubt hoped that Captain Holland would be able to effect something much less than a need to use guns. He had little time, for the Admiralty insisted on the completion of the mission before nightfall on the 3rd.

Foxhound entered the large bay at 6 a.m. Force H was visible from lookout points on the headlands, a presence that was completely unexpected by the French who had been preparing to demobilise their ships in accordance to the articles of the armistice. To go inside the inner harbour Holland signalled "The British Admiralty has sent Captain Holland to confer with you. Request permission to enter harbour," and the message was passed from the Port War Signal Station to Admiral Gensoul. There was no reply so Holland signalled again:

"The British Admiralty has sent Captain Holland to confer with you. The British Navy hopes their proposals will enable you and the valiant and glorious French Navy to be by our side. In these circumstances your ships would remain yours, and no one need have any anxiety for the future. A British Fleet is at sea off Oran waiting to welcome you." Holland was an excellent choice as emissary; he had once served as Naval Attaché at Paris and was known to Gensoul and other French commanders.

After waiting for about an hour, *Foxhound* was allowed to enter the harbour, a pilot was sent aboard to guide her to a berth near the *Dunkerque* but Holland insisted on keeping the destroyer just outside the anti-submarine nets so that she could get away if necessary without being impeded. Admiral Gensoul, however, refused to go out in his barge to meet Holland, sending instead Lieutenant Dufay who spoke perfect English and who showed a certain diplomatic ability. He also knew Holland quite well.

As Gensoul expected, Lieutenant Dufay was handed an ultimatum – the one drafted by the war Cabinet – which he took to the Admiral whose immediate reaction was to order his ships to prepare for battle. Then he made contact with the French Admiralty, relaying the various options outlined in the ultimatum but excluding the one that offered the Fleet sanctuary in the West Indies or America. Perhaps he thought it was of little importance in relation to the other options, or he may have overlooked it, or he may not have wanted the Germans to know of it – and he was sure that they would be reading his signals.

As far as the first two options were concerned – joining Britain to fight on, or taking their ships to a British port – to accept either would have been a direct violation of the armistice: it was not within the province of the Navy to contravene any of the armistice articles. Neither did Gensoul intend to scuttle his ships nor be the first to open fire. He did not expect to find his problem eased in any reply to his signal to Vichy: 'A British force comprising three battleships, an aircraft carrier, cruisers and destroyers off Oran. Ultimatum issued: Sink your ships within six hours or we shall compel you to do so by force. My reply: French ships will meet force with force."

69

What would have happened if Gensoul had decided to sail his ships to the West Indies or the United States? There was still a goodly sized bargaining Fleet at Toulon for French politicians to use in their argument with the Nazis; there were ships at Dakar, Casablanca and Algiers, ships whose future was also being decided that morning, Gensoul imagined. To sail out would be the less sanguinary move, one which most men would have chosen if they did not have the French Navy discipline bred in them. Admiral Darlan was the man to decide on any change in the plan.

At 9 a.m., when the French warships were already showing signs of getting up steam in their boilers and the tropical awnings were being taken down, Dufay brought a message down to where Holland waited in one of *Foxhound's* boats. There had been no invitation to come ashore for breakfast; they were treating each other as strangers. "The assurances given to Admiral Sir Dudley Pound still remain unchanged," wrote Gensoul in his message. "In any case, under no circumstances will French warships be allowed to fall intact into the hands of the Germans or Italians. In view of the substance and form of the unmistakable ultimatum presented to Admiral Gensoul, the French warships will defend themselves by force." Dufay told Holland that the Admiral would not give up his ships to anyone at any time, anywhere, any way, and without further orders from the French Admiralty. All systems in the Admiral's brain had clamped into stubbornness and anger.

Holland wanted to keep the talks going and to do so he and two other British officers, Spearman and Davies, climbed into Dufay's barge. There the thoughts behind the British Government's action were explained to Dufay to convey to Gensoul: the Germans and Italians would break the terms of the armistice whenever it was convenient to their purposes to do so, and without any effect on their conscience. But all French staff officers knew how important the Fleet was to France in her forced acceptance of

70

the armistice, and they knew too that the Axis forces could never be quick enough to take a French warship before it was scuttled. It was becoming obvious to Holland that Force H would have to open fire on his old friends; Dufay later said that the Captain appeared to be most discomfited. His conversation was reported to Gensoul who next sent his Chief of Staff, Captain Danbe back with Dufay and a written reply:

"Admiral Gensoul can only confirm the reply already given. Admiral Gensoul is determined to defend himself with all means at his disposal. Admiral Gensoul draws the attention of Admiral Somerville to the fact that the first shot fired would have the practical effect of putting the whole French Fleet against Britain, a result which would be diametrically opposed to that sought by the British Government." Admiral Gensoul was also keeping an eye on Force H, steaming about at sea on its police beat, and on the RN aircraft scouting over the base and harbour.

Back in *Foxhound* Holland communicated all his information to his Admiral in the *Hood*, and from his headquarters Gensoul repeated the same to his Admiralty. Because the ships in the harbour were raising steam, Somerville ordered Holland to signal that the French squadron would not be permitted to leave the harbour; Gensoul signalled back, "I have no intention of sailing. I have signalled my Government from whom I am awaiting instructions. Do not create an irreparable situation." Somerville informed the Admiralty that he was ready to open fire; he sent aircraft from *Ark Royal* to mine the harbour's entrance channel and informed Gensoul that the ultimatum would expire at 2 p.m. GMT. At one o'clock *Foxhound* signalled, "If you accept the proposals, hoist a square flat at the mainmast of *Dunkerque*; otherwise we shall open fire."

Half an hour before deadline Admiral Gensoul prolonged the negotiations by signalling that he was prepared to receive Admiral Somerville's representative for an

71

honourable discussion. Both Admirals knew that negotiations could not last longer than that day, apart from the fact that the British force could not stay in that position while the war continued in the Mediterranean. The deadline had passed when Captain Holland stepped aboard the battleship for his interview with Gensoul, who was obviously trying to prolong the negotiations in the hope that the British would understand his situation and believe that the French Navy's honour would be at stake if any of its ships passed into enemy hands. He could convince Somerville and the Cunninghams and Captain Holland perhaps; there was no hope of convincing Churchill and his Cabinet. Nor did Gensoul expect any help from his own Admiralty whose Chief was at Clermont-Ferrand; the Government was moving from Bordeaux to Vichy and were at Nérac when Gensoul made contact with Admiral Le Luc's headquarters radio.

Le Luc had no need to confer with politicians on what had to be done: if Gensoul joined the British or scuttled his ships to please them, or fled to the West Indies without permission the Germans might occupy the whole of France and claim all her overseas territories. And why didn't the British trust the good word of Admiral Darlan who had so often told them that the Fleet would never be taken? He made a signal from his radio truck alerting all squadrons in the Mediterranean: "Get under way ready for action. Report to the Admiral in *Dunkerque* at Oran." The message was repeated in plain language so that the Royal Navy – and the Germans – would pick it up. General Maxime Weygand later said that when the French Council of Ministers met that afternoon to discuss the challenge at Oran "it would appear that Admiral Darlan whether deliberately or not, or whether he was aware of them or not, I do not know, did not in fact inform us of all the details of the matter at the time. It now appears that the terms of the British ultimatum were less crude than we were led to believe, and suggested a third and far more acceptable alternative, namely, the departure of the Fleet for West Indians waters." Churchill tried to find an explanation of this omission but failed.

Was the escape clause sent to Darlan, or did Gensoul deliberately ignore it? Later, people like Weygand said that the Oran squadrons may well have been allowed to obey the British demand and take their ships across the Atlantic. And later, too, people like Churchill admitted to misunderstanding over Darlan's intentions relating to the sentence in the paragraph of the 2nd July demand which read, "The Council of Ministers declared on 18th June that before capitulation on land the French Fleet would join up with the British Navy or sink itself." Misunderstanding, said Churchill, was caused by their paragraph:

"As late as June 14 Admiral Darlan had favoured the idea of sending the French Fleet to British ports in certain eventualities, but by June 18 he had become Minister of Marine. Thereafter the new French Government under Marshal Pétain would not give the specific assurance demanded by the British. The second sentence in this paragraph therefore no longer represented the position of the French Government. In the crisis this last-minute change was not appreciated by the Admiralty officials concerned."

"The distress of the British Admiral and his principal officers was evident from the signals which had passed," Churchill wrote in his history. "Nothing but the most direct orders compelled them to open fire on those who had so lately been their comrades. At the Admiralty also there was manifest emotion. But there was no weakening in the resolve of the War Cabinet. I sat all the afternoon in the Cabinet Room in frequent contact with my principal colleagues and the First Lord and First Sea Lord. A final signal was despatched at 6.26 p.m."

That signal, read by Somerville, was no doubt meant to dispel any indecision. The Admiral certainly did feel distressed but no more than Holland who was shown by Ad-

73

miral Gensoul the French Admiralty's message of 24th June, the message signed by Darlan and sent to all commanders: that the armistice clauses were accepted only on the condition that the French Fleet would remain French, under the French flag, with reduced French crews, and would definitely remain French thereafter; the Admiralty considered that these arrangements would not be prejudicial to British interests.

Surprised at this information, Holland could understand more fully why Gensoul had stretched the confrontation from morning to after five o'clock in the afternoon.

Impatiently, and worried about Le Luc's order to the rest of the Fleet to get under way ready for action, the Admiralty signalled Somerville: "Settle the affair quickly or you will have reinforcements to deal with."

It is highly likely that Gensoul could have been persuaded to disarm his ships at Mers-el-Kebir and Oran if he had gone out to meet Somerville that morning and had taken with him Darlan's order, for as the last deadline approached he was deciding to disarm his ships. Somerville had established the deadline – "If none of the British proposals are accepted by 1730 BST I repeat 1730 BST it will be necessary to sink your ships," a message received on *Dunkerque* a couple of hours earlier. The coastal batteries had been alerted, a group of fighter aircraft readied and the crews were loading shells into ships' guns, although no ship had got under way in case it should provoke the British into opening up.

Now it was too late. Gensoul could not act on his own without orders from his Admiralty.

Lieutenant-Commander Davies reported that "Action Stations sounded as Holland's party went down the gangway to the barge that took them back to *Foxhound*," and "Some of them actually waved to us as we left, and both Holland and I felt certain they hadn't the slightest idea what was going on. I clearly remember too the Officer of the Watch on board the *Bretagne* saluting us smartly as we passed. Ten minutes later, the shells from our battle wagons blew her to pieces!"

Chapter 6

THE ATTACK

A FEW minutes before 6 p.m. the British battleships were heading on a 70-degree course, making a short easterly run at 20 knots, while two submarines, *Pandora* and *Proteus* were posted outside Oran and Algiers; Captain Holland and his party were still in *Foxhound*'s boat on their way to the destroyer, and the French sailors did not appear to be in any great hurry or to have their seaward-facing guns traversing to a common direction.

From some 17,000 yards out, in a position north-north-west of Mers-el-Kebir, the battleship *Resolution* opened fire with her 15-inch guns, the salvo flying over *Foxhound* and the small boat in which the British emissaries heard the rush of enormous shells before they crashed down on the breakwater pier area. The ships at Mers-el-Kebir were the important target and those at Oran were ignored. Lieutenant-Commander Davies said that "the effect of those shells bursting on the breakwater was far more devastating than a direct hit. The jagged stones they hurled up in all directions cut like scythes through the men crowding the upper decks of the ships, killing scores of them and maiming hundreds more." It was the finish of what Gensoul had believed: that until 6 p.m. on 3rd July, the sentiments of the French Fleet had been one hundred per cent pro-British. Now they were ninety-nine per cent anti-British.

The high heat of the desert-fed air had dropped as the evening approached but it was still hot as French sailors worked feverishly at guns and controls while the ships began moving in the confined space between the breakwater and the shore. The battleship *Provence* took only a minute and a half to get away her first salvo of 340mm shells – her biggest – and was forced to fire between the masts of Admiral Gensoul's flagship. As she fired, *Provence* manoeuvred into line behind *Strasbourg* and *Dunkerque*, with *Bretagne* in the rear. The leading battleship took only seconds to get under way, time enough to avoid an accurate salvo from the *Hood* falling directly into her vacated berth, one fragment of steel flying up to cut the flag halyards; *Strasbourg* kept going ahead, gathering speed as she steamed through the Mers-el-Kebir channel on a course that would take her to the open sea.

British destroyers laid a smoke screen down between Force H and the land, a haven for one destroyer which came up to challenge the *Strasbourg* only to be frightened off with her mighty broadsides. The magnetic mines dropped earlier by the *Ark Royal*'s Swordfish aircraft were miraculously avoided as the battleship increased her speed to fifteen knots and sailed out, accompanied by five of the large *contre-torpilleurs* whose gun power was far superior to that of the British destroyers; *Le Terrible* and *Volta* fired at one destroyer attack and kept them at bay. The five large destroyers had been berthed close to the shore opposite the breakwater and beyond the first target area. There the *Dunkerque* was hit as the huge shells rained down, first by a 15-inch shell as she was beginning to move out and soon afterwards by a 15-inch salvo. Her guns stopped firing when she was paralysed by serious damage to her electrical system, and then her captain headed her towards the shore away from the target area. Before power was cut from her guns she had managed to fire back at the British line, straddling the *Hood*, an Admiral-to-Admiral piece of shooting.

There was smoke everywhere – screens from Royal Navy destroyers and French ships, and smoke from the battleship *Bretagne* which was also hit before she could get away from the breakwater. Sinking by the stern, she burst into

77

flames that reached her magazines and blew her apart in one mighty explosion that echoed back from the nearby hills. She then rolled quickly over and went down smoking and steaming, taking with her nearly a thousand officers and men.

Sweating in the turrets of the British battleships, gunners continued to load and fire the hundred-ton guns with their 15-inch projectiles. As they knew, the four capital ships were together in a row and closest to the lighthouse end of the breakwater when the firing began. A fifth large ship, the 10,000-ton seaplane tender *Commandante Teste* armed with only 100mm (3.9-inch) guns, completed the row at the breakwater. She got away from the berth and was still intact when the *Provence* was hit so heavily a fire broke out in the aft section and she was beached with her nose resting on a ledge five fathoms deep near the shore; her forward guns pointed the wrong way and her aft guns were near the fire. *Commandante Teste* could have moved out of the dangerous area but her captain took her close to where the *Bretagne* lay wrecked to pick up survivors.

In the channel a tug got in the way of the large destroyer *Mogador* which was unluckily hit by a 15-inch shell when she stopped to avoid the tug. She was hit aft where depth charges exploded and blew her stern off, right up to the after engine room bulkhead, yet she managed to turn away from the channel and anchor in shallow water near Oran while fire-boats came up with hoses.

Sixteen minutes was the time elapsed from the first salvo to the last that was fired into the Mers-el-Kebir target area. There were other explosions at sea after Somerville ordered the firing to cease: submarines were trying to get at the British battleships and were being warned off with numerous depth-charge attacks by destroyers. In the sixteen minutes of heavy, accurate fire on the almost stationary ships, whose range from the Royal Navy guns had been carefully estimated during the day, the French lost one battleship sunk, two damaged and beached and a heavy destroyer badly damaged.

The sun was low in the sky when Admiral Somerville ceased fire in answer to Admiral Gensoul's signals that his battleships still in port were out of action. Somerville replied that unless he could see the ships sinking he would again open fire; and he was prepared to send another two hundred tons of shells into the Mers-el-Kebir base. The "battle" was not yet over for the *Strasbourg* which had steamed at full speed north-east along the coast under the protective guns of the batteries at Gambetta, Espagnole and Canastel, with *Volta* and *Le Terrible* making sorties out to ward off British destroyers, and *Tigre* and *Lynx* staying close to the battleship.

Force H had made a turn to head west for about twenty minutes after firing so that by the time *Strasbourg* was on her way north-east Force H was well behind – some fifteen miles – when she passed Point Aigulle and began to turn more towards the east. A sister ship to the *Dunkerque*, her main armament of two four-gun turrets on the foredeck only fired 13-inch shells which each gun could every twenty seconds, the shells weighing 1,258 pounds. Maximum range with these guns was almost 46,000 yards – 26 miles – but if she were to take on the battleships of Force H she would have to turn around and spoil any chance of escape. At top speed she could make 31 knots or cruise comfortably at 28 knots. *Volta* and *Le Terrible* could make 42 knots and 45 knots respectively, when they were new, and were armed with 5.5-inch guns.

Somerville took his ships out on the north-westerly course under a smoke screen protection against the six-inch fortress guns firing too accurately for his comfort. When *Strasbourg* was reported to be escaping with a destroyer escort he called up *Ark Royal* to direct her aircraft onto them. The carrier had been manoeuvring into wind to take on and fly off her aircraft and at one stage was on a divergent course with the fleeing battleship until warned by one of the aircraft. It would have been fitting to call off the attack then – as *Foxhound* had been allowed to leave Mers-el-Kebir bay unscathed – but the Swordfish biplanes of the Fleet Air Arm carried out an attack as the ships were passing Point Aigulle. Their torpedoes missed then and missed again in two later attacks made when the battleship was some twenty miles from land and forty from her shell-wrecked berth.

Captain Louis Collinet had no more trouble after that and arrived in Toulon before lunch the following day, the *Strasbourg* and her accompanying destroyers receiving a tumultuous welcome from all the sailors at the base. It had been quite an achievement to get away from a standing start while being fired on with 15-inch shells, get through a mine-field, elude a strong force of battleships and avoid three attacks by torpedo-planes. *Hood* had given chase until dark then was recalled by Somerville – who expected a "colossal raspberry" from his chiefs for not nailing the Frenchman and allowing it to sail to a port more easily available to the Germans – if they had a mind to take over the Toulon base.

That afternoon of the 4th, the submarine *Pandora* had a chance to sink *Commandante Teste* but was unable to get into firing position in time as the ship sailed to Algiers and the protection of better coastal defences. The colonial sloop *Rigault de Genouilly* was unlucky when she made the voyage to sanctuary, being sunk by the submarine *Proteus* as she sailed towards the harbour. The rest of the destroyers and sloops which were not attacked at Oran sailed without incident to Algiers.

The historians of the French Navy outline the profitless results of the attack on Mers-el-Kebir: "From a purely military standpoint, Force H had accomplished only a part of its objectives: one old battleship sunk, another dis-abled, and the *Dunkerque* damaged to an extent which at that time could have been easily repaired. On the other hand the encounter almost resulted in what may have been predicted by Gensoul and feared by the British themselves; a complete about-face by the entire French Navy, which up to then had been 100 per cent pro-British. Darlan, feeling it a personal insult that his word had been doubted, was blazingly indignant over this new "Copenhagen". His first reaction was to send out orders, at 2000 on July 3, to attack all English ships met. The next day he obtained from the German armistice commission a cancellation of all requirements that French ships be disarmed. But on July 5 he substituted for the order of the 3rd a new and wiser order, warning that, "All British ships approaching to within less than 20 sea miles of the French coast are open to attack." This warning was widely broadcast immediately. It looked as though Hitler was given a victory without having fired one German round.

Three days after the attack *Ark Royal* was again sent to Mers-el-Kebir: reports had been received that the *Dunkerque* was but slightly damaged. At dawn she was attacked by Swordfish aircraft carrying torpedoes; the planes flew in through anti-aircraft fire from all the ships in the harbour and from guns on shore, and missed with all attacks except one – and that was a ricochet: a patrol vessel loaded with depth charges was torpedoed near the battleship which was holed by the explosion, killing 150 men and bringing the total death toll up to 1,300.

*

A few days before the end of June, Admiral Godfroy at Alexandria had been ordered by the French Admiralty to up-anchor his squadron and leave the British base. The British Commander-in-Chief, Sir Andrew Cunningham, had also received orders: to request Godfroy to keep his ships in port, a request Godfroy acceded to since the armistice had not been signed between Germany and France.

Cunningham was on excellent terms with the French Admiral whose ships had been operating with the Royal Navy for some time, and when Cunningham received the same orders that took Somerville to Mers-el-Kebir he felt the same anxiety about having to use force.

Godfroy was on board his flagship, the 10,000-ton heavy cruiser *Duquesne*, when he received news of the attack on Gensoul's ships, and naturally he prepared for action, angry and disappointed with his ally. Steam was raised in his ships and guns were readied for action. Go out fighting, ordered his Admiralty, and don't surrender ships to the British. In the early light of the following day he could see the guns of battleships and cruisers pointing towards his cruisers as he waited for the expected negotiations to begin. He had already sent a message to Cunningham withdrawing his promise not to take his ships out of port and stating that he was determined to go out even if it meant having to fight his way.

The situation was very different from Mers-el-Kebir, and in the wide bay of Alexandria both groups of ships were sitting ducks. The British advantages were that they had the shore batteries, the land-based fighters and bombers, bigger-gunned ships and, if necessary, field artillery to use. The battleship *Lorraine* mounted eight 340mm guns which would create a lot of havoc before she was silenced.

At 7.30 a.m., when tension was at its highest and British crews were standing by at first readiness, an Italian air raid developed – one of those high-flying hit-and-run raids that hardly ever interrupted a poker game on ship or shore. The Italian Savoia-Machettis were nevertheless good target practice and on this occasion both British and French ships opened fire on the raiders. Perhaps with the real enemy attacking them all, the French relaxed; at least they gave a great display of not caring, as Admiral Godfroy noted in his memoirs:

"These dispositions [washing decks and scraping rust,

etc.] kept busy an important part of the crew for whom an occupation was necessary. No better work could be found than that laid down by the standard routine – washing down decks, shining brightwork, etc. This cool carrying on of ship's routine astonished the British, who talked about it a long time afterward. Admiral Cunningham's sailors, tensely waiting behind their armour, could see their French comrades continuing their usual shipboard life as if nothing unusual were occurring, and as if they did not even see the guns of the British Fleet trained on them." Sailors went swimming from the *Lorraine*, and Godfroy ordered all ships' guns to be layed simply fore and aft. No one could shoot at ships in that state of apparent unreadiness.

If Gensoul and Somerville had only been able to meet! Cunningham and Godfroy reached a sane agreement after British captains of warships visited their opposite numbers among the French – the *Ramillies* captain calling on the *Lorraine*'s captain, the *Malaya*'s captain calling on the *Suffren*'s captain – after which all the French captains went on board *Duquesne* to discuss the situation with their commander. Cunningham had made sure that all French officers and men were informed of the British demands, and the crisis ended when Godfroy went on board *Warspite* to agree to a settlement: there would be no attempt to seize the French ships by force, and they would unload their fuel oil, store all breechblocks and torpedo firing pins at the French consulate, and all crews would remain on their ships.

Three days later the agreement was written in a formal statement and signed by the Admirals:

French ships would not be scuttled and would be maintained in their present condition.

They would not be seized by the Royal Navy.

Personnel would be reduced to a complement to be agreed upon; men released from duty would be repatriated.

Those remaining on board would not attempt to leave Alexandria or engage in hostile actions against the British.

The Royal Navy would ensure an adequate supply of rations, medical stores and clothes to the ships.

The agreement would be revised if the ships were seized or used by Germans or Italians.

*

Up to now no French ship or submarine had gone out looking for British warships to attack, but then they were still confined under German demands while the armistice talks continued. The only hostile act originated by the French was an air attack on Gibraltar, and that was a mild gesture of protest and caused little damage. The French military and political leaders were angered over the Mers-el-Kebir attack, and so was General de Gaulle who broadcast to the world on the BBC, saying that he had learned with grief and anger of the shelling, and he hoped the British would not portray "this hateful tragedy as a direct naval success." De Gaulle realised that he would lose much support for his cause as a result of the action, and he was correct: recruiting figures dropped to a very low mark. In his broadcast he did not mention all the actions but as "Oran" and "Mers-el-Kebir" were the names that hit the headlines around the world they were what everyone thought about.

There were, however, some dramatic moments at Dakar – the French West African port in Senegal – and at Casablanca.

The new, uncompleted battleship *Richelieu* was based in the steamy West African port where she was out of everyone's way as long as she stayed there, but she didn't, for according to Admiral Auphan the French Admiralty considered the political atmosphere too vague and too unsettled; both military and civilians were inclined to favour continuing the war and the presence of British warships in the area encouraged that attitude: towards the end of June she set out for Casablanca and was still at sea when the orders issued by the War Cabinet were enforced on 3rd July.

The captain of HMS *Dorsetshire* received this signal that night:

"*If* Richelieu *sails and proceeds north she is to be shadowed.*

"*If she is about to proceed towards West Indies you are to make every endeavour to destroy her by torpedo attack and if this fails by ramming repeat ramming.*"

That signal suggests that the offer to Gensoul to take his ships to the West Indies was insincere. *Dorsetshire* had been shadowing the battleship for some days, and after reporting this to Vichy she was ordered back to Dakar.

At the time HMAS *Australia* was engaged in convoy escort duty until 3rd July when she was ordered by the Commander-in-Chief South Atlantic, Vice-Admiral D'Oyly Lyon – whose flagship was the armed merchant cruiser *Edinburgh Castle*, based at Freetown – to sail immediately to rendezvous with *Dorsetshire* and the aircraft carrier *Hermes* off Dakar. During the passage north in company with *Hermes*, D'Oyly Lyon signalled that French submarines had been ordered to attack British naval forces off Dakar, and that French submarines and aircraft there were to be destroyed on sight. *Dorsetshire* reported that she had sighted two submarines and had sunk or damaged one of them.

Obviously a strong force was not required to cope with *Richelieu* which had never fired her main battery of 380mm guns and her anti-aircraft battery was not in working order, but with the other operations against the French likely to produce hostile reaction everywhere it was decided that *Dorsetshire* should have the assistance of the Australian cruiser and the carrier. Those two ships made a rendezvous with the British cruiser at dawn on the fifth and for the next two days patrolled off Dakar, *Hermes* maintaining an air patrol over the harbour. Early the next morning a French aircraft flew over to attempt a bombing but its stick of bombs fell harmlessly into the sea, and *Hermes* launched her torpedo-bombers to attack the virtually harmless battleship in Dakar's harbour, without any personal approach being made to the ship's commander.

Meanwhile, during the night an abortive attempt to damage the *Richelieu* with depth charges was made by a daring group of British sailors under the command of Lieutenant-Commander Bristowe: they would sneak into the harbour in the *Hermes* motor-boat and fix the battleship without all the loss of life that would be caused by bombing or shelling; the idea being to drop depth charges under her stern if she was stationary or in front of her if she was moving. With blackened faces in a black-painted motor-boat the crew were fortunate to make the harbour, having cracked one engine head and flooded the deck with a spilled drum of oil. With a muffled engine they slid over the boom and after visiting a couple of wrong warships found the *Richelieu*; they were challenged several times on the way. The depth charges were thrown overboard near the stern of the battleship and the motor-boat retreated, again challenged and, when the charges exploded, chased by a couple of French patrol boats that unbelievably did not open fire. However, what they believed to be exploding charges was not their cluster for the water had been too shallow for the detonator to work. They all returned safely to *Hermes* which sent out its Swordfish; one of them scored a torpedo hit aft, damaged the rudders and propeller shaft, flooded three after compartments, leaving her immobilized for a year.

If Britain wished to alienate French West Africa this was certainly the way to do it. As Auphan said, with this torpedo, Franco-British relations began to split wide apart.

And militarily, *Richelieu* was not an immediate threat: she had never fired her main battery and if she ever were in fighting trim and was taken over by the enemy Britain would have had ample warning – had Britain maintained good relations with France and been able to maintain consular officials at Vichy and French territorial capitals. But the day after the attack on Mers-el-Kebir, Pétain's government broke off diplomatic relations with Britain, whose consular officials were cabling in: "shall I leave my card with French colleagues; should I fly flags on 14th July?"

Five days after the attack the French Chargé d'Affaires in London advised the Foreign Secretary that in view of the British action against the French Fleet, "the French Government find themselves compelled to recall their diplomatic representatives." The Foreign Office's man in Tangier cabled in cypher, "regrettable incident of Oran . . . providing serious reactions . . . de Gaulle and Muselier should immediately broadcast, explaining the necessity for Britain's action at Oran and saluting the Air Patrol."

Why the Oran Air Patrol should have been "saluted" is a mystery – the French aircraft were partly demilitarised but the British Skuas and Swordfish were obsolete, although the two-seater Skua dive-bomber/fighter was the first to shoot down a German aircraft in the war. The Fleet Air Arm aircrews on *Ark Royal* were mostly inexperienced as they proved when they attacked *Strasbourg* – the bombers missed and the Fairey Swordfish biplanes, waiting until the battleship was silhouetted against the setting sun, came down to sea-level and dropped their torpedoes outside the destroyer screen instead of penetrating first. As a result the battleship got clean away into the gathering darkness. The aircrews tried hard but did not have their hearts in loosening torpedoes at the fine French ships and there was no jubilation on board the *Ark Royal* when they returned from any of their attacks.

Had it not been for the fact that France was already in a terribly confused mess as a result of the barbarian's victories, France would have replied to the attacks with more violence than she did. Two days after "Oran", His Majesty's Consul-General at Tangier sent a Most Immediate signal to the War Cabinet:

"French Military Attaché has just told me that,

(a) French Air Force which bombed Gibraltar this morning is based at Port Lyautey and that their immediate objective is HMS *Hood*.

(b) All French warships left Casablanca at 12.30 p.m. yesterday except *Jean Bart*.

(c) *Richelieu* has sailed from Dakar.

(d) French Navy are out for anti-British submarine campaign *à l'outrance*.

The submarine campaign "to the finish" was called off, and so was the Cabinet's plan to attack *Jean Bart* at Casablanca, taking advice from Admirals North and Somerville – at last. Why attack a battleship which might never be completed in its present berth? The Admirals were advised that the policy regarding the French Navy was reviewed and a decision made not to take any further action in French colonial or North African ports, reserving "the right to take action" in regard to French warships proceeding to enemy controlled ports. "Pending further instructions ships must be prepared for attack when meeting a French warship but should not fire the first shot." Advised of the Admiralty's decisions, the French accepted for the time being that their ships were under blockade, and a useless naval war between them was avoided. There were, however, to be further British blunders in this regard.

*

John Masefield wrote of the sailors and seamen – and they included many French: "Courage godlike and of hearts of gold, Off Dunkirk beaches in the little ships". After Oran it was a time for regret and sadness. Churchill said this in a speech in the House of Commons on 4th July:

"It is with sincere sorrow that I must now announce to the House the measures which we have felt bound to take in order to prevent the French Fleet from falling into German hands. When two nations are fighting together under long and solemn alliance against a common foe, one of them may be stricken down and overwhelmed, and may be forced to ask its Ally to release it from its obligations. But the least that could be expected was that the French Government, in abandoning the conflict and leaving its whole weight to fall upon Great Britain and the British Empire, would have been careful not to inflict needless injury upon their faithful comrade, in whose final victory the sole chance of French freedom lay, and lies.

"As the House will remember, we offered to give full release to the French from their Treaty obligations, although these were designed for precisely the case which arose, on one condition, namely, that the French Fleet should be sailed for British harbours before the separate armistice negotiations with the enemy were completed. This was not done, but on the contrary, in spite of every kind of private and personal promise and assurance given by Admiral Darlan to the First Lord and to his Naval colleague the First Sea Lord of the British Admiralty, an armistice was signed which was bound to place the French Fleet as effectively in the power of Germany and its Italian following as that portion of the French Fleet was placed in our power when many of them, being unable to reach African ports, came into the harbours of Portsmouth and Plymouth about ten days ago. Thus I must place on record that what might have been a mortal injury was done to us by the Bordeaux Government with full knowledge of the consequences and of our dangers, and after rejecting all our appeals at the moment when they were abandoning the Alliance, and breaking the engagements which fortified it.

"There was another example of this callous and perhaps even malevolent treatment which we received, not indeed from the French nation, who have never been and apparently never are to be consulted upon these transactions, but from the Bordeaux Government. This is the instance. There were over 400 German air pilots who were prisoners in France, many of them, perhaps most of them, shot down by the Royal Air Force. I obtained from M. Reynaud a personal promise that these pilots should be sent for safe keeping to England, and orders were given by him to that effect; but when M. Reynaud fell, these pilots were delivered over to Germany in order, no doubt, to win favour for the Bordeaux Government with their German masters, and to win it without regard to the injury done to us. The German Air Force already feels acutely the shortage of high-grade pilots, and it seemed to me particularly odious, if I may use the word, that these 400 skilled men should be handed over with the sure knowledge that they would be used to bomb this country, and thus force our airmen to shoot them down for the second time over. Such wrongful deeds I am sure will not be condoned by history, and I firmly believe that a generation of Frenchmen will arise who will clear their national honour from all countenance of them.

"I said last week that we must now look with particular attention to our own salvation. I have never in my experience seen discussed in a Cabinet so grim and sombre a question as what we were to do about the French Fleet. It shows how strong were the reasons for the course which we thought it our duty to take, that every Member of the Cabinet had the same conviction about what should be done and there was not the slightest hesitation or divergence among them, and that the three Service Ministers, as well as men like the Minister of Information and the Secretary of State for the Colonies, particularly noted for their long friendship with France, when they were consulted were equally convinced that no other decision than that which we took was possible. We took that decision, and it was a decision to which, with aching hearts but with clear vision, we unitedly came. Accordingly early yesterday morning, 3rd July, after all preparations had been made, we took the greater part of the French Fleet under our control, or else called upon them, with adequate force, to comply with our requirements."

And on Bastille Day the Prime Minister included these sentiments in a broadcast address:

"During the last fortnight the British Navy, in addition to blockading what is left of the German Fleet and chasing the Italian Fleet, has had imposed upon it the sad duty of putting effectually out of action for the duration of the War the capital ships of the French Navy. These, under the Armistice terms, signed in the railway coach at Compiègne, would have been placed within the power of Nazi Germany. The transference of these ships to Hitler would have endangered the security of both Great Britain and the United States. We therefore had no choice but to act as we did, and to act forthwith. Our painful task is now complete. Although the unfinished battleship the *Jean Bart* still rests in a Moroccan harbour and there are a number of French warships at Toulon and in various French ports all over the world, these are not in a condition or of a character to derange our preponderance of naval power. As long, therefore, as they make no attempt to return to ports controlled by Germany or Italy, we shall not molest them in any way. That melancholy phase in our relations with France has, so far as we are concerned, come to an end.

"Let us think rather of the future. Today is the fourteenth of July, the national festival of France. A year ago in Paris I watched the stately parade down the Champs Elysées of the French Army and the French Empire. Who can foresee what the course of other years will bring? Faith is given to us, to help and comfort us when we stand in awe before the unfurling scroll of human destiny. And I proclaim my faith that some of us will live to see a fourteenth of July when a liberated France will once again rejoice in her greatness and in her glory, and once again stand forward as the champion of the freedom and the rights of man. When the day dawns, as dawn it will, the soul of France will turn with comprehension and with kindness to those Frenchmen and Frenchwomen, wherever they may be, who in the darkest hour did not despair of the Republic."

This comment from a Royal Navy man should be included; it was written by Captain S. W. Roskill in his book *The Navy at War 1939–1945*:

"The necessity for this violent action by the Royal Navy against its former Ally has been hotly debated ever since that fateful day. What can be said with confidence is that three British flag officers involved in it – Admiral Sir Dudley North on shore at Gibraltar, Admiral Cunningham at Alexandria, and Admiral Somerville himself – all viewed the government's orders with something approaching horror; and all three believed that, given time for negotiation, a peaceful solution could have been found. Admiral North indeed expressed such a view to the Admiralty in writing, and that report provides the background to what became a *cause célèbre* in British naval and political circles after the war; for in the following October, after the failure at Dakar, he was relieved of his command."

Comment on the attacks at Mers-el-Kebir and Dakar vary from source to source and it is worthwhile noting what Auphan and Mordal wrote for the US Naval Institute. (When the Royal Navy fired on French ships it was "the English", not the British):

"As far as the French Navy was concerned, the day of July 3 had two consequences of major importance.

"The first was to isolate the Navy further from the military and the remainder of the country. The Germans were by now counting their prisoners – one and a half million –

sorting their booty, and infiltrating themselves into the administration of the Occupied Zone. The suffering mass of Frenchmen began to be aware of the rigors of occupation. They were thinking a great deal more about what was happening at home than about those battles in faraway African ports of which the average citizen understood nothing. The sailors, was the popular thought, were wrong; it was not England, but Germany, that was the enemy. 'I cannot believe,' one of Gensoul's acquaintances was to say later, 'that the English were the first to fire.'

"The second consequence of that day was the return to Toulon of the bulk of the French naval forces. If it had not been for the aggression of the British, the principal French squadrons would have remained in North Africa, out of reach of the Germans. Under the original applications of the armistice, there would have been only one naval force based in European France, and that would have been merely a 'police division', made up of light craft. But with the ports of Casablanca, Mers-el-Kebir, Algiers, etc., all directly on the coast, at the mercy of another British attack, the remaining capital ships of the French Navy – including the *Dunkerque* when she was temporarily repaired – took cover under the protection of the powerful coastal batteries of Toulon. Thus they came nearer to the German forces in the Occupied Zone."

In the British official history of the Second World War, *The War at Sea 1939–45 Vol. 1*, the author, Captain S. W. Roskill wrote: "It can be argued indefinitely that, had the British alternatives been presented before a display of force was made, or had more time been allowed for negotiation, on normal diplomatic lines," the clash may have been averted; and that "French officers still in London were not fully informed about the trend of affairs in their own stricken country, about the naval clauses of the armistice terms so recently accepted, nor about French intentions with regard to their fleet.

"In neutral countries the reaction was not unfavourable. It seemed to be readily realised that Britain, fighting alone to secure her life-lines, simply could not afford to allow her very existence to be jeopardised by any uncertainty or weakness in her handling of so dangerous a situation."

The world was ready to believe Britain – even, it seems, Frenchmen who listened in to BBC broadcasts by de Gaulle and Churchill. According to the secret papers released from Foreign Office security, President Roosevelt knew and approved of the plan so there could be no criticism after the event from that quarter, and the British Commonwealth was sympathetic to the official British line. The Prime Minister's later comment was this: "The elimination of the French Navy as an important factor almost at a single stroke by violent action produced a profound impression in every country. Here was this Britain which so many had counted down and out, which strangers had supposed to be quivering on the brink of surrender to the mighty power arrayed against her, striking ruthlessly at her dearest friends of yesterday and securing for a while to herself the undisputed command of the sea. It was made plain that the British War Cabinet feared nothing and would stop at nothing. This was true." It was hardly true that the French Navy had been eliminated; or that it had made any move meant to inspire fear.

Chapter 7

FIFTY DESTROYERS

IT is now possible to surmise that had Britain not antagonised France by first of all distrusting her admirals and then bombarding her battleships at Mers-el-Kebir, the war may have ended earlier than it did: the French could have resisted the German invasion of Tunisia and when the Unoccupied Zone was invaded the Toulon fleet may have joined the Allied Navy, as the armistice terms would have been broken. Perhaps the War Cabinet members would in any case have felt that a show of defiance should have been made. But at the time Britain's greatest need, if she were to survive the air battles from June to September, was an enlargement of her Fleet, especially in her destroyer squadrons. If it had been possible then, to exchange bases in the Western Hemisphere to the United States for fifty old destroyers, would the attacks on the French Fleet ever have taken place?

When it was obvious that France was going down under the blitzkrieg, the first thought was not of fighters but of warships to keep the enemy off Britain's shores, and that urgency could have influenced the people at Downing Street when they thought of their warship numbers compared with what the Germans might have if they could seize the French warships. And it was then, before the fall and before Dunkirk, that Churchill told the American Ambassador, Mr. Joseph Kennedy, that what Britain most urgently needed was a loan of thirty or forty old destroyers. If the loan had been effected that month or in June it is doubtful if the subsequent hasty decisions over the French would have been made, but it takes a long time to effect a loan and to prepare a lot of old First War destroyers for action. The following account of that transaction illustrates the close ties that existed between Britain and the United States and which were a great encouragement to Britain in her darkest hour.

Having served twice in the Admiralty, Churchill signed himself "Former Naval Person" when he sent this telegram to President Roosevelt:

"Although I have changed my office, I am sure you would not wish me to discontinue our intimate private correspondence. As you are no doubt aware, the scene has darkened swiftly. The enemy have a marked preponderance in the air, and their new technique is making a deep impression upon the French. I think myself the battle on land has just begun, and I should like to see the masses engage. Up to the present Hitler is working with specialised units in tanks and air. The small countries are simply smashed up, one by one, like matchwood. We must expect, though it is not yet certain, that Mussolini will hurry in to share the loot of civilisation. We expect to be attacked here ourselves, both from the air and by parachute and air-borne troops in the near future, and are getting ready for them. If necessary, we shall continue the war alone, and we are not afraid of that.

"But I trust you realise, Mr. President, that the voice and force of the United States may count for nothing if they are withheld too long. You may have a completely subjugated, Nazified Europe established with astonishing swiftness, and the weight may be more than we can bear. All I ask now is that you should proclaim non-belligerency, which would mean that you would help us with everything short of actually engaging armed forces. Immediate needs are, first of all, the loan of forty or fifty of your older destroyers to bridge the gap between what we have now and the large new construction we put in hand at the beginning of the war. This time next year we shall have plenty. But if in the interval Italy comes in against us with another hundred submarines we may be strained to breaking point. Secondly, we want several hundred of the latest types of aircraft, of which you are now getting delivery . . . .Thirdly, anti-aircraft equipment and ammunition, of which again there will be plenty next year, if we are alive to see it. Fourthly . . . to purchase steel in the United States . . . Fifthly, we have many reports of possible German parachute or air-borne descents in Ireland. The visit of a United States squadron to Irish ports, which might well be prolonged, would be invaluable. Sixthly, I am looking to you to keep the Japanese quiet in the Pacific, using Singapore in any way convenient. The details of the material we have in hand will be communicated to you separately . . ."

*

America in 1939 was more isolationist than in the pre-1914 days, the people remembering the bungling and slaughter of the First World War, yet the rise of Nazism and the threat of war induced Congress to legislate for an increase of armament. When war broke out, however, the allocation of funds was still meagre until the European events in May brought the shock of realisation that if Germany knocked out Britain and her fleet the United States could be threatened from both oceans. President Roosevelt then asked for an increase in the appropriation from 142 million dollars to at least one billion dollars.

As far as the Allies were concerned, the most important legislation was the passing of a revised Neutrality Act in October, 1939, giving the Franco-British Allies access to American war supplies on a cash-and-carry basis, yet maintaining for the US a moral status of neutrality. Aircraft, for example, would be flown to the Canadian border and rolled across the frontier that happened to be on an airfield; European ports were "out of bounds" in this new game while the Pacific and Indian Oceans, the Mediterranean, African and Canary Island ports were open.

At the end of the earlier conflict the United States Navy had retained numerous warships including a lot of rusty, top-heavy destroyers, whereas Britain had scrapped over thirty of her older destroyers; both countries had about the same number of battleships, and Britain possessed a greater number of aircraft carriers and cruisers. Behind any lack of armaments at that time lay America's immense manufacturing resources and the genius of mass production methods.

From the day Churchill made his request for American ships, to the end of the evacuation from Dunkirk, the Royal Navy had lost almost half of its home waters and Atlantic destroyer strength, either by sinking or serious damage, and many others were slightly damaged. At that time the world was wondering if Britain could survive, could fight back, and it was Churchill's determined and aggressive attitudes, reflected in his speeches, that encouraged the world to accept the fact that the fight would go on. Britain, of course, was not alone: she had a very loyal and willing Commonwealth readily sending men and what arms they had to the British Isles and to the Middle East; few, however, had more than a few cruisers and destroyers to offer. If the worst happened and Britain were invaded, the Royal Navy would have done exactly as the French had done: sent her ships to a dominion, in her case, Canada.

In reply to the request for the destroyers, the first on the list of Britain's needs, Roosevelt had cabled back: ". . . As you know, a step of that kind could not be taken except with the specific authorization of the Congress, and I am not certain that it would be wise for that suggestion to be made to the Congress at this moment [May]. Furthermore, it seems to me doubtful, from the standpoint of our own defence requirements, which must inevitably be linked with the defence requirements of this hemisphere and with our obligations in the Pacific, whether we could dispose even temporarily of these destroyers. Furthermore, even if we were able to take the step you suggest, it would be at least six or seven weeks at a minimum, as I see it, before these vessels could undertake active service under the British flag . . ." There were greater prospects of being able to send aircraft and anti-aircraft guns and ammunition.

Churchill's answer to this cable expressed his disappointment and a forecast of what terrible things might lay ahead:

". . . I am very sorry about the destroyers. If they were here in *six weeks* they would play an invaluable part . . . you must not be blind to the fact that the sole remaining bargaining counter with Germany would be the Fleet, and if this country was left to its fate no one would have the right to blame those then responsible if they made the best terms they could for the surviving inhabitants. Excuse me, Mr. President, putting this nightmare bluntly. Evidently I could not answer for my successors, who in utter despair and helplessness might well have to accommodate themselves to the German will . . ."

M. Reynaud too could not answer for his successors; the French Fleet was France's remaining bargaining counter . . .

In six weeks from that 20th May telegram Britain would need every warship she could possibly get if the enemy invaded, and whether some thirty squadrons of RAF Spitfire and Hurricane fighters could stop the Luftwaffe was also indeterminate. At that time, Churchill fully believed that the French Fleet would always be there to reinforce the Royal Navy; and later, at the end of the evacuation, he was forced to think in terms of a possible defeat and what would happen under such circumstances. He cabled the Canadian Prime Minister, Mr. Mackenzie King, that the Americans must not be allowed to view too complacently the prospect of a British collapse, "out of which they would get the British Fleet and the guardianship of the British Empire, minus Great Britain." He added that although Mr. Roosevelt was their best friend, no practical help had so far come from America – "they have not even sent any worthy contribution in destroyers and planes, or by a visit of a squadron of their Fleet to Southern Irish ports. Any pressure which you can apply in this regard would be invaluable." When the message was passed on to Washington the American leaders were alarmed and distressed, as they also had been when they were informed of the attack at Oran two days earlier, and they were more alarmed when they heard of the enormous losses of arms, equipment and destroyers caused by the evacuation from Dunkirk. A sadder state of affairs they did not know was that a German air force of some 4,000 planes were poised to attack England and her 700-strong fighter defence.

And there was the question of money. The war now meant for America that the Depression that began at the beginning of the last decade was just about over: America was arming and the British Purchasing Mission had behind it a gold and securities backing of three thousand million dollars, and the first big chunk of cash went to buy aeroplanes, mainly P-40 fighters. Britain was destined to come out of the war broke, and the American economy enriched, but in 1940 Britain was prepared to spend every last farthing if it meant remaining unconquered and if possible victorious. The man Britain chose to spend its treasure was a British-Canadian, Arthur B. Purvis, and the American who handled most of his country's deals was the US Treasurer, Henry Morgenthau. "Surplus arms" was a term often used then in dealings between the two and it usually meant field guns, machine-guns, mortars, rifles and ammunition which the United States might need for defence but which could be declared surplus for the purpose of helping Britain.

Once all the legal and political difficulties had been worked out and the price fixed, American arsenals across the country were opened up and hundreds of freight cars rolled in towards the Army docks. Soon after the OK to sell was given and the laden trains arrived, thousands of men were employed to move the equipment onto lighters and out to British merchant ships in Gravesend Bay. Towards the end of June the first ship arrived in Britain with millions of rounds of ammunition, thousands of rifles and machine-guns and a few dozen field guns. The .30 Lee-Enfield rifles would be a useful addition to the shot-guns and pitch-forks of some Home Guard units as well as partly-equipped Territorials. The equipment was old but sound and cheap, and during the first month of the Battle of Britain the ground forces received over seventy thousand tons of equipment, including enough field guns to equip several regiments of artillery, an important factor in the event of an invasion.

The United States Army chiefs, especially General Marshall, were most sympathetic towards Britain's cause and Britain's need, one of the reasons why the military equipment was on its way so quickly once the go-ahead signal was made. The United States Navy however, was ingrained with a different attitude, one based primarily on a traditional and sometimes bitter rivalry with the Royal Navy. Fortunately, Admiral Harold Stark, the USN Chief of Naval Operations, was above such pettyness as he exhibited when he sent back fifty dive-bombers to the manufacturers explaining, as did the US Air Corps to facilitate sales to the RAF, that he would wait for an improved version of the aircraft. The same trick could not be applied to old destroyers: that deal was much more involved politically.

*

Correspondence between the Prime Minister and the President increased during June, the major topic always being the destroyers, and the ever increasing need for them: "The Italian outrage makes it necessary for us to cope with a much larger number of submarines, which may come out into the Atlantic and perhaps be based on Spanish ports. To this the only counter is destroyers. Nothing is so important as for us to have the thirty or forty old destroyers you have already had reconditioned. We can fit them very rapidly with our Asdics, and they will bridge the gap for six months before our war-time new construction comes into play. We will return them or their equivalents to you, without fail, at six months' notice if at any time you need them . . ."

The President had already mentioned to an official that he did not think the old warships would be of much use anyway, and that an Act of Congress would have to be passed to sell them; and Admiral Stark was not keen on letting them go. There was also the delicate matter of popular opinion – the voters' reaction to letting part of the US Fleet out of the country's control – and whether the lending of the ships would be an acknowledgement of America's involvement totally against the Axis Powers.

More messages arrived from Britain – from Churchill, from Ambassador Kennedy, from the US Naval Attaché – and from Purvis and the British Ambassador, Lord Lothian. On 26th June, King George VI wrote to the President: ". . . we are in urgent need of your older destroyers to tide us over the next few months. I well understand your difficulties, and I am certain that you will do your best to procure them for us before it is too late. Now that we have been deprived of the French Fleet – to put the least unfavourable interpretation on the present position – the need is becoming greater every day if we are to carry on our solitary fight for freedom to a successful conclusion." By now the President was inclined to agree with the idea of sending the ships and may have done so, if he had the approval of Congress.

The political machinery guiding naval affairs was managed by the Senate Naval Affairs Committee – the decision-makers of the US Navy's size, composition and expenditure – and that Committee were not only against releasing destroyers, no matter how old or rusty, and were objecting to letting Britain have twenty new cash-sale MTB's: "a grievous wrong," said an influential Committee member, Senator Walsh from Massachusetts, adding that it was only by accident that he and his fellow committeemen learned of sales of naval aircraft, vessels and munitions. The MTB's were cancelled, and Walsh quoted the United States law passed in 1917 forbidding the sale of any vessel of war to a belligerent nation while the United States was still neutral. The politicians were showing isolationist tendencies again and at the same time the Services chiefs were looking to defence, contemplating the seizure of French and British colonies in the West Indies. It began to look as if all material help might be cut off from Britain, and her Caribbean possessions could be occupied by United States forces in their need to cast their defending aircraft and ships to stronger positions near the Panama Canal, that most vulnerable and important communication link for the US Navy between the two oceans' fleets.

Thus the bargaining medium came to more prominence in the thoughts regarding destroyers. The possible acquisition of British islands in the Caribbean and British Honduras had already been mooted in Senate debates and the suggestion passed on to the British Government. Fortunately, for the resultant bargaining necessity, Britain said "No".

The next hurdle in the chase was the American elections, a not so difficult hurdle with both major factions proclaiming, in their majorities, that they were all for helping Britain; and meanwhile two Anglophiles, Frank Knox and Henry Stimson, had joined Roosevelt's administration, one as Secretary of the Navy, the other Secretary of the Army.

Both were keen to send large forces to Britain, and Navy Secretary Knox, who had been one of Teddy Roosevelt's rough riders in Cuba, was the kind of fiery man Britain needed on her side to hurry things along.

Towards the end of July the War Cabinet decided to offer America the use of naval base facilities in the Caribbean. The Royal Navy had lost four destroyers and another seven were damaged in the previous ten days, a fact that Churchill quickly sent to Roosevelt: "All this in advance of any attempt which may be made at invasion. Destroyers are frightfully vulnerable to air bombing, and yet they must be held in the air bombing area to prevent sea-borne invasion . . . I am confident, now that you know exactly how we stand, that you will leave nothing undone to ensure that fifty or sixty [the number kept rising] of your oldest destroyers are sent to me at once . . . in the long history of the world this is a thing to do NOW . . . The air is holding well, We are hitting that man hard . . . But the loss of destroyers by air attack may well be so serious as to break down our defence of the food and trade routes across the Atlantic . . . I am sure that, with your comprehension of the sea affair, you will not let this crux of the battle go wrong for want of these destroyers."

The hour of decision was approaching: the Americans wanted the bases, Britain wanted the destroyers, and at last Frank Knox decided that the matter should be brought up at a Cabinet meeting in the White House early in August and that any legislation concerning the transfers should have the approval of both the President and his opposing candidate in the elections – Wendell Wilkie. As the Republican nominee, Wilkie would be able to influence the anti-transfer people in his party, and there were more among the Republicans than among the Democrats. The Cabinet unanimously agreed that the destroyers should be handed over on the condition that the bases were made available for use by the US Navy and that in the event of Britain being overrun, the Royal Navy would withdraw to America, and, supposedly continue the fight which would eventually involve the United States.

Churchill wanted a go-ahead at full steam, whereas it was with brakes on in the US Secretary of State's department: it all had to be done legally and with all the details written out – words for aircraft *and* ships to use the bases, Pan-Am to have the lease of a site adjacent to the Trinidad airport, rights for training flights to Newfoundland, bases at Jamaica, British Guiana and Trinidad. Britain's requirements in return were: twelve flotillas each of eight destroyers – a total of *ninety-six* – complete with torpedoes, reserve equipment and ammunition; twenty modern motor-torpedo-boats with torpedoes or depth-bombs and ammunition; fifty Catalina flying boats and several dive-bombers; and 250,000 more rifles. Then there was the legal snag – the law about selling ships of war to a belligerent nation – and some American representatives were worrying about public opinion despite the existence of a campaign to swing opinion in favour of the transfer.

A week after the Cabinet meeting Roosevelt advised Churchill that it "may be possible to furnish . . . as immediate assistance at least fifty destroyers", and a few planes for "war testing", if Britain were willing to agree with the conditions previously mentioned, and the bases at Newfoundland, Bermuda, the Bahamas, Jamaica, St. Lucia, Trinidad and British Guiana bought or leased for ninety-nine years by the United States. On 15th August, the biggest day of battle to date in the skies over England, Churchill wired back his acceptance of the terms, and his gratitude.

The details took some time to be sorted out, both in governmental and diplomatic processes, until on 3rd September, Admiral Stark signed the documents which certified that the destroyers were not essential to the United States national security and could go. That day Churchill was able to announce to the House of Commons that "no

doubt Hitler will not like this transference of destroyers . . .
There will be no delay in bringing the American destroyers
into active service; in fact, British crews are already meeting them at the various ports where they are being
delivered."

*

"Even as little as four months ago any Anglo-American
Agreement of this nature would have been regarded as an
example of one-sided American assistance to Britain and
denounced as such by a large part of American opinion.
But events have brought clearer sight. It is no diplomatic
hyperbole for the British Government to speak of their
'sympathetic interest in the national security of the United
States'; it has become our own sheet anchor. And there
are few in America who do not now recognise England as
their only line of defence that is fully manned and in fighting trim. There could not be a clearer example of genuine
reciprocity than this exchange.

"With all this background of mutual advantage it is all
the more satisfactory that in the details of the arrangement
there is no hint of charity. Great Britain is giving full value
for what she receives; the price of fifty destroyers for a
century's lease of six bases might even be called cheap. Indeed the only free gifts are from Britain to America. One
of these free gifts is the northern group of bases. The other
is the solemn assurance from the British Government that,
come what may, the Royal Navy will be neither surrendered nor scuttled. It is important that the meaning of this
should be fully appreciated. It means that in certain un-
likely, but not impossible, circumstances, the inhabitants of
Great Britain would abandon themselves to occupation and
starvation and would consent to be blockaded by their own
fleet rather than leave the way to the New World open to
the Nazis. The fact that no patriotic Englishman would

have it otherwise does not in the least diminish the value to America of this pledge. 'England expects every American to do his duty' was the bitter jibe of a few years ago; in dead earnest it has been changed to 'America can count on every Englishman doing his duty.' " That comment from the *Economist* accurately summed up the situation.

With their bottoms scraped free of barnacles, the vintage destroyers were handed over, fully equipped with fresh American victuals and armament, ammunition, spare parts and other stores; they were difficult to handle at first and it took some time for their new crews to get used to their old-fashioned idiosyncracies, such as the 4-inch guns which tended to fire themselves when raised to extreme elevation, and there were breakdowns and collisions: one of the first handed over, renamed HMS *Churchill*, was damaged in an accidental ramming by one of the others which were all named after towns common to both Britain and America. During the following months and years the destroyers served valiantly on escort duty in the various seas, sinking submarines and some being sunk by the enemy. *Churchill* survived until January, 1945, when she was sunk by a U-boat in the Arctic; and *Campbeltown*, altered to the appearance of a German destroyer, was used to ram the outer gate of the Normandie Dock in the famous commando raid on St. Nazaire, in March, 1942, the action that earned her commander, Lieutenant-Commander S. H. Beattie, the Victoria Cross. The 20-knot ramming broke the dockyard gate, the crew left the ship to be captured, and while Beattie was being interrogated the explosives packed into the prow exploded, blowing the gate apart and killing a lot of Germans.

*

Looking back, it is interesting to note that one of the conditions under which Britain obtained the destroyers could be related to the conditions laid down by the Germans in their armistice with France. The Germans demand that *"the French war fleet, except that part permitted for the protection of French interests in its colonial empire, is to be assembled in ports to be disarmed under German or Italian control."* The American President's request was that if the waters of Great Britain became untenable for British ships of war, *they would not be turned over to the Germans or sunk, but would be sent to other parts of the Empire for continued defence of the Empire.*

The possibilities of the aftermath of a successful German invasion are intriguing: *if* Churchill was captured or killed while smoking a cigar over his brandy during an air raid, and *if* a less defiant successor agreed to an armistice clause that Royal Navy ships should be demilitarised in Empire ports, would the United States, when her time came to fight the Axis powers, have sent battleships to knock out tied-up British ships?

Chapter 8

THE FFNF AND DAKAR

THE first serious consequence to all that ridiculous shooting was that when de Gaulle donned a pith helmet and set out for Dakar he was heading for a hostile, instead of hospitable, shore. Not only had the attacks aroused animosity, there was antagonism everywhere, from small trading ships to large cruisers and the French Admiralty. France was endeavouring to supply herself from overseas territories with a great variety of essential foods and materials, and to suffer interruption, confiscation and inspection of a blockade was very irritating. The Royal Navy was also looking at Spanish ships trading around the French zones of the Mediterranean but usually the small traders were allowed to pass. Although Churchill was all for "keeping the screws" on Dakar and "not allowing any West African trade that the Navy can stop to pass into the Mediterranean from the Atlantic, whether escorted or not," he "saw no reason why we should embroil ourselves about any traffic in the Mediterranean, whether from Spain or Vichy," as he wrote in a note to the Foreign Secretary.

A greater prize than seized contraband was Dakar and the French colonial empire – to be brought back to the conflict against Germany – and Churchill was more than willing to back with British ships de Gaulle's wish to establish the Free French movement in West Africa. There was also the threat from Germany of grabbing Dakar and providing a major strategic threat to British trade around the Cape – a vital route now that Italy was in the war and was a threat with her submarines and bombers to every convoy passing the Straits of Gibraltar. Again Dakar was to be a disappointment to the visitors – the Royal Navy and the FFNF.

To begin with that part of the French Navy whose soul was never in danger of being lost – the Free French Naval Forces – FFNF: Indirectly it quickly came into being because of Admiral Darlan's disagreement with the Naval Officer commanding the Marseilles base – Vice Admiral Emile Muselier, the result of the disagreement ending in Muselier's early retirement a couple of weeks before war broke out. He sat on the sidelines during the "phony war" until he saw what was happening to the French Fleet as a result of the armistice and escaped from Marseilles on a collier to Gibraltar. There he was fortunate in finding a ship which had already done some good work against the Germans – the freighter *Rhin*, just returned from carrying French underwater specialists of the French Secret Service to Las Palmas in the Canary Islands. The swimmers had placed limpet mines against the hull of the German freighter *Corrientes*, blowing her up and escaping unscathed.

Another piece of good fortune was finding in the *Rhin*'s radio operator an ally dedicated to avoiding the armistice and carrying on France's fight against the enemy. He was Claude Péri, a man who preferred to seek action than to wait about while French military politics resolved their confused intentions; when he got the *Rhin* to England he ignored de Gaulle and offered his ship and his services to the Royal Navy. Before that happened there was indecision on his ship at Gibraltar, some of the crew not wanting to join his and Muselier's defiance of the armistice and Darlan's plan for his country's ships, and Péri was obliged to force all but six of the crew to leave.

Under Muselier's command, the *Rhin*, three other cargo ships and the French Navy auxiliary vessel *Président Houdance* formed the nucleus of the naval equivalent of de Gaulle's army. The General welcomed the Admiral when he arrived by air in London from Gibraltar, on 30th June, and offered him the command of his "Legion's" naval and air forces. It was Muselier who, realising that there must be a distinction between the national emblem at the mastheads of the French Navy ships, under Pétain's and Darlan's control, and his own ships, decided on an ensign featuring the Cross of Lorraine over a white diamond on a blue field. Thus the inspiring symbol came to be used by all Free French.

Perhaps to the French scheming is irresistable – more so in times of high drama and in the phlegmatic English atmosphere – and perhaps they are easily aroused to suspicion, or were in those years when their heads of State were so untrustworthy and governments so unstable. De Gaulle brought to England some of the ingredients of French administration that caused conflict among Frenchmen as well as his allies, the most aggravating being his security service. In his memoirs, Admiral Muselier blames that service's chief for bringing to a crisis the strained relations between de Gaulle's staff and the staff of the FFNF. Muselier was arrested, on 2nd January, 1941, by Scotland Yard inspectors and a Royal Navy intelligence officer on trumped-up charges which included alleged collusion with Vichy. After ten days, first in a prison then under Admiralty supervision, he was released and was offered an apology signed by Anthony Eden for the Government's involvement in what was really a French domestic squabble. Muselier resumed his positions as Commander of the FFNF and Free French Naval Commissioner.

Another naval officer who sought direct action against Germany instead of waiting for a miraculous restitution of his country was Lieutenant François Drogou, submarine commander stationed with his division at Sousse, Tunisia. When he heard of the armistice terms he took matters into his own hands and sailed his boat, *Narval*, to Malta where he later declared his allegiance to the free and operated under orders from the Royal Navy. On its third patrol *Narval* was lost when it hit a mine off the Tunisian coast.

There were, of course, many others like Péri, Drogou

111

and Muselier, but few of them could command the destiny of crews and ships; and there were the 20,000 French sailors, 12,000 from ships in English ports, who had fought before the armistice or escaped when France fell. However, of the latter only a few hundred were initially recruited to the FFNF, none of whom came from the crews of ships in port. Naturally, the blame for this dispirited interest lay with the British action at Oran Bay, also partly with the emigré leader, of whom hardly anyone knew, when he announced that the men at Vichy – and Pétain and Weygand were old national heroes – "are but tools subject to the will of the enemy," and solemnly declaring, "in the name of France that the Empire must not comply with their disastrous orders."

There was resentment at being interned and they were susceptible to anti-British propaganda which possibly emanated from those who did not trust de Gaulle. The two good Frenchmen, Auphan and Mordal, who carried on the fight offered this explanation:

"Here and there were sincere and generous souls for whom these questions presented no problem at all. They either decided to continue the war to the death against the Germans, or they chose to remain in the path of discipline and obey a government dignified by the names of Pétain and Weygand.

"But there were many, many others who did not find the issues so plainly resolved. Some would have remained with the FFNF if they had not families in France to look after – families from whom they had no news. Some looked forward to being completely free of any of the military services with their traditional bonds of discipline. Still others were without any ties whatsoever, and were attracted by the promise of a new adventure. And there were officers who took the considered stand of refusing to consider any change until they could no longer do anything for the men of their crews who were so dependent upon them."

An appeal was sent to the men by Muselier's FFNF after the attacks at Oran and Dakar:

"We appeal to the youth, to those who have faith, to those who believe that our country has not merited its present humiliation; to those who believe in the immortal destiny of the French people; to those who are prepared to act, and if necessary, to die, in order to create a new France ... If in spite of this appeal, you should all abandon us, we shall none the less maintain our faith in a final victory ... We shall remain proud of having been those who swore not to return to our native land until after having driven out the enemy; not to return to our harbours except in our victorious ships – those same ships which have never ceased to fly the eternal flag of France."

And this was their reply, which might have been written under a waving tricolour while a band played the Marseillaise:

"In order not to permit our ships to fall into the hands of the enemy, our crews accomplished prodigies. We left behind us only wrecks. We carried out that day, without doubt, the greatest sacrifice that can be made in a lifetime. Then we came to the English ports, seeking hospitality and friends – still expecting to supply ourselves and repair our ships, in order to continue the fight.

"Then the armistice was signed. We experienced the same inner feelings of rebellion as you did when the news of the defeat was officially acknowledged. But we ascertained that the orders of the Government were being carried out by the Navy and the empire. We have taken the decision to do likewise ...

"We are neither vanquished nor desperate men. Our faith in a final victory is equal to yours. England continues the war. Her insular position permits her to do so. We fervently hope that she will be victorious. But, we desire that a new France emerge from that victory. The Navy, which has not been defeated, which has remained intact and sound, which has, in short, an élite service, must have a major part in the task of restoring France while waiting to re-enter the fight for the final liberation of our country . . .

"Although we have chosen to follow different paths, we fervently hope that we shall meet again some day. May it be within the bosom of a strong, independent, and united France, restored to its social, national, and Christian ideals by the energy of her sons, the virtues of her race, and the tribulations of her ordeal."

How the authors of that reply expected their Navy to play a major part in restoring France, without fighting the enemy who held most of Western Europe in his grip, is a mystery. By the end of the year almost 3,000 men joined the few hundred FFNF, and the rest of the sailors were re-patriated to French North African ports. During the next two years more than 2,000 enlisted from those who escaped from France, from overseas territories and from French ships captured at sea. There were never enough French sailors to man all the French ships, both warships and mer-chantmen, seized in British ports, offered voluntarily, or captured on the high seas.

Paris and *Courbet*, two old battleships built before the First World War and still retaining large four-faced clocks on top of their tripod foremasts, added during refitting in the twenties, were not worthwhile additions to the Royal Navy's sea-going fleet and were used at Plymouth and Portsmouth as anti-aircraft batteries, wearing both the French ensign and the Union Jack. *Courbet* was also depot ship for the FFNF which in the early autumn commissioned the large destroyers *Léopard* and *Triomphant* with full complements of French crews. Newer ships presented less problems than the older for which there was a lack of met-ric spares.

Rear Admiral George Thierry d'Argenlieu, who had been for a time after the first war a Carmelite monk, was given *Léopard* and *Triomphant* for his Free French Naval Forces of the Pacific in 1942. *Léopard* had shared a U-Boat kill before being damaged in a collision with a British corvette and spending a couple of months in the South African repair yards at Simonstown. Her shells fired at the Vichy battery on Reunion Island helped persuade the colonials to end their resistance and accede to the Free French. After a diversion to the Indian Ocean she was lost when grounding during a convoy escort duty along the coast of Cyrenaica, in 1943. *Triomphant* escorted convoys between New Caledonia and Australia then spent most of 1942 undergoing repairs in Sydney. Her commander, Philippe Auboyneau, replaced Muselier as Commissioner of the FFNF when that admiral again clashed with de Gaulle and ended up for a spell in a fortress.

The hardest working ships flying the Cross of Lorraine were six of the nine corvettes transferred to the FFNF from the Royal Navy. The six escorted convoys in the North Atlantic, two of them were sunk by U-boats while the corvettes sank at least three of the enemy submarines; two of the latter were sunk during the escort of Convoy HX-228 by *Aconit,* commanded by Lieutenant Jean Levasseur. The convoy was dogged by a U-boat pack during the night of 10th March, 1943, HMS *Harvester* rammed and slightly damaged one which *Aconit* finished off with a more effective ramming; then the following morning *Harvester* was torpedoed and sunk by a U-boat which *Aconit* detected and cut in two with her sharp bows. Altogether she completed thirty-four escort missions in the dangerous North Atlantic.

There were some 140 merchant ships, ranging from large transports to trawlers, of which about one third were manned by Frenchmen; a little fleet of great value when German submarines began to take a larger toll in the waters around the beleaguered island.

Two other warships, apart from the *Narval,* to join the Allies fully manned were the submarine *Rubis* and the colonial sloop *Savorgnan de Brazza*, and even then the *Rubis* had undergone the indignity of being forcibly seized until her commander decided to continue under the Free French Navy C-in-C. When all submarines had been re-called from the North Sea in June, *Rubis* had continued her excellent mine-laying operations, begun with the Royal Navy during the Norway campaign, operating until the end of June and getting a German sub chaser in its minefield laid in the Trondheim approaches. Under her original commander, Georges Cabanier – later to reach the rank of admiral – and then under Henri Rousselot, *Rubis* sank seventeen enemy ships during twenty-two patrols, an out-standing record by any standards.

The colonial sloop *Savorgnan de Brazza* also dis-tinguished itself in action, shooting down at least one German plane and making the Atlantic crossings as a convoy escort, and she was in the company of the *Président Houdance* and the sloops *Commandant Duboc* and *Commandant Domine* in the expedition to Dakar.

Three other submarines went back into service: *Minerve*, *Junon* and the large *Surcouf* with its battery of 8-inch guns. *Surcouf* was eventually recommissioned when the work unfinished at Brest was amazingly completed by her skilful crew and she was sent on several patrols in the Atlantic. When the Pacific war broke out it was decided that she would be of great value because of her size and fire power, in the Pacific, but on her way to Panama she was accidentally rammed at night by the American freighter *Thomson Lykes*.

Getting *Junon* and *Minerve* to sea was a lengthier job for they had been towed without spare parts to England. Early in the following year they began operations in the North Sea and when convoy PQ-17 was being attacked, *Minerve* was one of the submarines on picket duty between Bear Island and North Cape. Both were involved in searches for the *Tirpitz* and *Junon* carried British and Norwegian commandos to Norway – including those who destroyed the German heavy water production plant. When the French fleets were reunited these submarines were still active.

*

With both the Germans and the British requisitioning her ships in ports and at sea, France suffered severely in maintaining supplies and communications to herself and her empire; nevertheless she somehow managed to land a total of 4,400,000 tons of merchandise at her Mediterranean ports between the period of the armistice and the Allied landings in North Africa. Despite an order by the Germans that French ships stopped by the Royal Navy should be scuttled, only two steamers and two small vessels were scuttled out of 104 that were stopped, and of these forty-three were released or retaken – one by a crew who got their English captors drunk and locked up in a hold, another by a Vichy cruiser and two destroyers.

There were now two French Navies, one flying the flag with the Cross of Lorraine, the other the tricolour, and there was the awkward problem of their possible meeting at sea. Eventually it was decided that should ships of the two forces happened to pass each other they should both be ignored. Admiral Auboyneau's instruction to all FFNF commanding officers that no mention of either ships' meetings should be entered into either ships' logs was for a while effective. That high comedy could not last when the Vichy Government was forced to defend its empire against Allied intrusion made necessary by their war against the Axis powers.

The Pacific possessions had been quickly persuaded to accept de Gaulle's authority – despite a little trouble with New Caledonia where the Australian cruiser *Adelaide* was used to threaten the sloop *Dumont d'Urville* whose captain was a Vichy loyalist. He was allowed to sail his ship to

Saigon. Also in 1940 the Congo, Chad, Ubangi-Shari and the Cameroons changed their allegiance to de Gaulle and the Free French Movement. All it took was a little pressure and a little persuasion. Dakar, de Gaulle's idea of a Free French capital and the British idea of an extra port now that the Mediterranean situation was forcing much sea traffic to the East around the Cape, became the object of an Anglo-Free French move about the same time as the Vichy French decided to send three cruisers and three large destroyers to Dakar – to restore order in the Gulf of Guinea: at Dakar, 1,500 miles from Gibraltar and at Libreville, 2,000 miles farther south.

When the French force passed through the Straits of Gibraltar on the way to Casablanca, Admiral Sir Dudley North, in command at the Rock, adhered to instructions that "no opposition is to be made to the movements of French naval vessels unless they head toward a port occupied by the enemy." And in doing so he was relieved of his command and placed on the retired list.

When London and Gibraltar were alerted to the French move the battleship *Renown* and escorting destroyers were too late to intercept before the French ships arrived at Casablanca. And then Admiral Sir John Cunningham's force, escorting an expedition of 2,400 Free French troops and 4,000 British support troops, were too late to intercept when the French ships moved on to Dakar. Spanish newspapers leaked the news that General de Gaulle had left England and the Vichy people could rightly guess that he was with the force now operating from Freetown.

The Royal Navy managed to turn three ships from their journey to Libreville back to Casablanca, but then de Gaulle's plans went awry. His emissaries and undercover agents sent to Dakar were arrested and Commander d'Argenlieu was wounded as he made his way back to the *Savorgnan de Brazza*. The sloops *Commandant Duboc* and *Commandant Domine* were sent with a detachment of marines who were to land and incite the crew of the *Richelieu* to rebel against Vichy, and when the sloops were forced to retire after a couple of shots from the battleship, one of the sloop captains sent a very English type of telegram to *Richelieu*'s captain: it was not cricket to fire on the little sloop, and the two captains' children attended the same school in Brest!

Then de Gaulle sent threatening messages that if he and his force were not allowed to enter peacefully "the important Allied forces which follow me will take over responsibilities for the matter," a threat that brought fire from coastal batteries and a torpedo attack by a French submarine on a British cruiser which sank the sub. HMAS *Australia* hit the large destroyer *Audacieux* which was set on fire and beached. Governor-General Boisson signalled Cunningham that "France had entrusted me with Dakar. I will defend Dakar to the end."

On 24th September the naval action began with more severity, Cunningham's two British battleships firing some 160 of their biggest shells at *Richelieu* and other warships in the harbour. *Ark Royal* had already lost four aircraft and another two were shot down. On the following day a French submarine damaged *Resolution* with a torpedo hit and the other battleship, *Barham*, was hit by shell fragments. Auphan and Mordal assert that because the French Navy was able to let off steam at Dakar, Franco-British relations improved after the battle! At least they had the satisfaction of seeing a strong British force withdraw: Dakar defences indicated that to take the port would be too costly and it was decided to take the less formidable Libreville and gain control of Gabon. Thierry d'Argenlieu commanded the Free French naval forces and Colonel "Leclerc" (actually de Hauteclocque) was in charge of the military operation.

The land defences were slight, the native troops inadequate and the naval defence rested with the sloop *Bourgainville* and the submarine *Poncelet*. Both sides were saddened

119

when the *Poncelet*, damaged and brought to the surface by a British patrol vessel, went down with its commander who deliberately opened the sea cocks. Other captured Frenchmen were to be of great value to the Allied cause once the Navies were again united, but de Saussine, *Poncelet*'s commander, automatically went down with his ship in true naval tradition, an unnecessary waste of life.

Another disappointment was that inevitably the *Savorgnan de Brazza* fought its sister sloop, the former without part of its crew who had reinforced the troops on shore, and, after a twenty-minute fight was set on fire.

To most personnel, this and future battles between former Allies and compatriots were incomprehensible: de Gaulle, the British, Vichy, Darlan, Pétain and anyone was blamed, but the bitter fact was that the German-Vichy agreement, the forced armistice, was the prime cause; that and the fact that warfare itself is an expression of the primitive instability in all mankind.

*

The campaign against Syria emphasised the Vichy French dilemma. The attack by British and French forces was made ostensibly because German planes had landed there on the way to assist revolting Iraquis, although those flights had ended when the attack began. If Admiral de Laborde had had his way his Toulon fleet would have entered the fray, but to do so they would have been compelled to use Axis ports and that collaboration could have led to a military alliance with the Germans and Italians. And, as Auphan and Mordal explain, ". . . it was not really the British against whom France was defending Beirut; in actuality what France was doing was defending Tunisia against occupation by the Axis, which inevitably would have happened had France not made an effort to defend her territories at Syria and Lebanon. For by the protocol which Admiral

Darlan had been forced to sign with the Axis on May 27, the way to occupation of Bizerte and other African ports would have been opened to the Germans." However, if that had happened the French Navy would have either been scuttled or gone over to the Allies and probably the unoccupied zone would have been occupied by German and Italian troops.

The campaign began on 8th June and ended on the 14th July, 1941, when General Dentz, High Commissioner and C-in-C of the Levant, signed the armistice at St. Jean d'Acre, the old Crusader town. The small Vichy naval force that de Laborde did send across was no match for Admiral Sir Andrew Cunningham's force or the reserves he could commit if necessary. A Vichy heavy destroyer and a submarine were sunk, and a destroyer and a tanker were damaged; the British destroyer *Janus* was damaged with a hit on her bridge.

Before the Syrian battles, the country that had been "neutralised" was also in action in the Far East. There was an undeclared war with Siam whose battleships were put out of action by the 8,000-ton cruiser *Lamotte-Picquet*, a naval action which led to a peace negotiated by the Japanese. The Japanese had already taken advantage of France's handicapped position, demanding with threats the use of airfields in northern Tonkin and the right to station troops there. Then, after the Siam conflict, Japan blackmailed from France the strategically valuable port of Saigon and airfields in Indo-China, airfields from which Japanese aircraft were to fly out to sink the *Repulse* and *Prince of Wales*. Vichy fought the British over Syria yet gave in to the Japanese without firing a shot, understandable when the French Indo-China forces numbered only 30,000 and their old warships inferior to the enormous strength of Nippon.

*

Although the Japanese made no threatening move towards Madagascar after the Malaya invasion, it was possible that they would, so the British made a surprise attack before successfully landing to begin a slow conquest of the island. The sloop *D'Entrecasteaux* managed to get out of Diego Suarez harbour to bring fire to bear on the landing beaches. She was put out of action by planes from HMS *Indomitable*; two submarines returning from escort duty were sunk; and *D'Irberville* and *Glorieux* managed to get away to Dakar. So ended another naval action forced upon the French by their German masters. The aftermath of Madagascar was that French North African forces were more incensed than ever against the British and de Gaulle's Free French, a feeling expressed by the refusal of the majority captured in Syria to join the Movement. Soured by those events, they were determined to fight if the Allies attempted to land on French North Africa, even if Rommel's panzers did break through at El Alamein and forced the immobilised ships at Alexandria either to be scuttled or sail with the Allies. Thus, when Operation Torch was committed to action, Vichy France and her empire were ready to fight – from Pétain down to the lowest ranking sailors, soldiers and airmen.

General Mark Clark, Eisenhower's envoy to pro-Allied plotters, landed by submarine to make his famous "cloak-and-dagger" meeting on the Algerian coast, on 21st October, 1942. The "Group of Five", which included General Charles Mast, two colonels and two civilians, had not risked bringing senior army or naval officers into their plot for fear of being exposed. "The French," wrote Clark, "gave us locations and strengths of troops and naval units, told us where supplies, including gasoline and ammunition, were stored; supplied details about airports where resistance would be heaviest, and information about where airborne troops could be safely landed." The advance units of the

Torch invasion forces were already at sea, a fact kept secret from the plotters.

It was impossible to hide the movement of over a hundred transports and two hundred warships but Darlan believed that Dakar might again be attacked by part of the armada and that the rest of it would be going to Malta or Egypt. On 8th November the Allies went ashore at Morocco, Tunisia and Algeria, the reason being, as Roosevelt said in a message to Pétain, that "Germany and Italy intend to invade and occupy French North Africa." Pétain replied, "It is with amazement and sorrow that I learned this night of the aggression of your troops . . . You invoke pretexts which nothing justifies. You attribute to your enemies intentions which have never been translated into action. France and her honour are at stake. We are attacked; we will defend ourselves. It is the order that I am giving."

At that time, according to some evidence, Pétain and Darlan were secretly hoping for and approving an invasion of southern France; and the only way that France's honour was at stake was with her agreement with dishonourable Nazis. When the landings took place Darlan happened to be in Algiers. He had already been on an inspection tour of the North and West African territories and had returned to Vichy where, at a reunion held in Admiral Auphan's house, he had predicted an Allied landing in southern France sometime in 1943. The reason he returned to North Africa was merely personal: he had received news that his son, whom he had recently seen in Algiers and who was then expected to recover from being stricken with poliomyelitis, had suddenly taken a turn for the worse. The same night he had received news that another event was occurring on the Provence coast: General Giraud, who had escaped from a German prison camp in April, was picked up by an American submarine and eventually transported to Gibraltar.

In North Africa, the influence of General Mast and other

army leaders contributed to some reduction in the resistance to the Allied landings. But the Navy fought back. Shore batteries caused heavy casualties and frustrated the efforts of the British destroyers *Malcolm* and *Broke* to crash the Algiers harbour boom and land American Rangers. *Malcolm* was forced to withdraw and *Broke*, after four attempts, rushed through at twenty-six knots and berthed at the quay where the Rangers disembarked, before an old casement battery on the foreshore shot down a wall to shell the destroyer, forcing her to leave. The Rangers were captured and disarmed. Two French submarines attempted to interfere but were driven off.

At Casablanca, the coastal defence battery on Cap El Hank and the battleship *Jean Bart* fired on the American battleship *Massachusetts*, and her cruisers and destroyers, while a light cruiser, seven destroyers and three submarines sailed out of the port. The battery and *Jean Bart* were temporarily silenced and many merchant ships in the harbour were sunk by shelling and aerial bombardment. The escaped French force headed for the American transports where they were attacked by radar-equipped cruiser and destroyer escorts, and had their topsides strafed by Wildcat naval fighters: the *Fougueux* was swamped by the *Massachusetts'* 16-inch guns, the *Milan* was hit and beached, and the *Boulonnais* was sunk by shell and torpedo hits. The *Frondeur* which had been hit aft capsized the following day when the *Albatros* and *Primauguet* were also smashed out of action; only the destroyer *Alcyon* remained undamaged when the so-called battle ceased. The historians of this gallant but misguided group related that "It had suffered its martyrdom purely because of those higher values without which no country can continue to exist – loyalty, discipline, patriotism, respect for national unity." Those same qualities the Free Frenchmen believed applied more realistically to themselves.

During the late afternoon of the 8th, Admiral Darlan had

issued an order to stop fighting but, with directives also arriving from Vichy, the *Jean Bart*, her damaged turret repaired, again opened fire and continued to fire, although heavily shelled and bombed, until Admiral Michelier got it into his thick head that Darlan's order was valid.

As well as the three submarines which escaped, five more were already at sea and three more were sunk during the massive bombing of the harbour shipping. Four attacked American transports without success and *Sibylle* was lost. *Sidi-Ferruch* was later sunk by US planes, *Méduse* was hit and forced to beach herself at Cape Blanc, *Conquérant* was sunk by Catalinas and *Tonnant*, depth-charged for two days, was scuttled after the crew were taken on board a fishing vessel.

In *The French Navy in World War II* Auphan and Mordal wonder if the suffering, the sacrifices and the fratricidal combats were necessary. "The answer," they state, "is to be found in the varying objectives which the combatants were pursuing. On the Anglo-American side the losses suffered were the price paid to gain a foothold in Africa without running the very real risk of complete failure if they had consulted in advance with the French Government. On the French side, while the French defenders were in intimate agreement with their attackers about taking up arms once more against the Axis, they were equally convinced that any such agreement should have been made though the proper authorities, and not through any secret group of subordinates and civilians. It was because of this that the French Navy fought the very people whom they would most have preferred as friends."

Chapter 9

SCUTTLING AT TOULON

WHEN Admiral Darlan ordered the cease-fire on 9th November the Vichy Government countermanded it, and Field Marshal Kesselring sent troops from Sicily to Tunisia to where Rommel, defeated at El Alamein, was also hurrying. Two days later, while the British First Army advanced towards Tunis and the nearby naval base of Bizerte, German forces overran the unoccupied part of France, thereby breaking one of the conditions of the armistice agreement.

This was the moment when the French Fleet had an opportunity, as far as conscience and honour were concerned – as well as a practical one to fight the real enemy – to join the Allies. The Fleet's commander also had another good reason, if he needed it: Darlan, as Commander-in-Chief of the Navy, ordered him to bring the main French Fleet at Toulon across to North Africa. Laborde, a fiery, quick-tempered man, as so many of his generation of admirals seem to have been, nevertheless considered himself still tied to his oath of loyalty to his Chief of State, an oath which personally bound all officers on their word of honour to Marshal Pétain, an oath made in addition to the normal one of allegiance whenever France was involved in war. Darlan's authority failed with Laborde who waited for Pétain to send confirmation, but the morose old Marshal was waiting for the return of Laval to Vichy with a party of German negotiators.

Admiral Auphan, who had earlier been appointed Minister of the Navy, asked in a signal to Grand Admiral Raeder that the status of the French Navy be respected. Raeder replied with a long letter, including in part, "The conduct of the leaders of the French Navy at Toulon – Admiral Marquis and Admiral de Laborde, to whom I request you transmit the highest regard which I attach to their declarations – bears me out, as well as your letter, in that opinion [that it will not evade the task]. It is for that reason that it was possible to entrust the defence of Toulon exclusively to the French Navy."

He was, of course, lying: he did not trust the Navy as he was to prove. Again the French had an opportunity of at least leaving Toulon on the pretext of defending the base from positions on the open sea. Auphan reminded commanders of all ships of Darlan's old promise to the British – that the ships must be scuttled if there was any chance of them falling into German hands. There was still the matter of keeping up the pretense of maintaining the armistice with the Axis who could, and later did, commit greater atrocities than shooting innocent hostages. These frightful, criminal and sadistic acts in occupied France had brought a great agony to the people there, as all the people of the south knew. Laval convinced the Ministers that Hitler, whom he had spoken to in Munich, would not consent to enter into any commitments with France, and that the Germans were still winning the war.

While Laborde and Marquis (the Maritime Prefect of Toulon) fruitlessly awaited a positive directive from Pétain, and while Auphan endeavoured to get the Ministers to make a change of policy so that the Fleet could be sent away from the danger of being commandeered by the old enemy, the Germans asked the Admirals whether they were prepared to defend Toulon against Allied attacks or whether they preferred to be taken over by the German army. Vichy undertook to defend Toulon against the Allies, at the same time secretly letting Darlan know that both Pétain and Laval approved of his taking over the functions of High Commissioner in North Africa in place of Weygand who had been arrested by the Gestapo.

A few days later the Germans broke their word and set in motion the events which were to make Toulon a scene similar to Pearl Harbour – without gun fire and without bombers and fighters diving out of the sky. French troops stationed in the Toulon area were ordered by the Germans to move out, as were French aircraft from adjacent airfields; German troops moved into Hyères to occupy the naval air base; ships were seized at Sète and Port Vendres; and all ships in Marseilles were placed under German guards.

Perhaps Laborde was now regretting that he had answered "*Merde!*" to Darlan's request to move his ships to Dakar, for the German intent was obvious. Not only had they made the notable moves about Toulon and at other ports, they were also bringing up a contingent of sailors.

Both admirals at Toulon commanded ships: Laborde's formed the High Seas Fleet comprising the new battleship *Strasbourg*, 3 heavy cruisers, 2 light cruisers, 10 heavy destroyers and 3 other destroyers; and Marquis commanded the old battleship *Provence*, a seaplane tender, 2 destroyers, 4 torpedo boats and 10 submarines. Also, there were the damaged battleship, *Dunkerque*, 2 cruisers, 8 heavy destroyers, 6 other destroyers and 10 submarines decommissioned under the armistice terms and crewed by maintenance staff. Thus there were 64 important warships as well as numerous light craft – chasers, patrol vessels, sloops and mine-sweepers, a Navy larger than those possessed by most nations of the world.

The more worthwhile ships were tied up at wharves or adjacent to those tied up. *Dunkerque* was one five ships of in the large dry docks, and the naval yards extended over an area more than a mile wide and a half-mile deep. Ashore lay the main arsenal. There were outposts to be passed by intruders but the main impediment to human movement was a high wall with only two gates. The Germans planned to take the dockyards with a surprise move by an army group travelling up the Nice road on motor-cycles while another three groups, including men from the despicable and cowardly "Das Reich" Division, seized the peninsula and its coastal batteries and the actual town. When the move did take place the only Frenchman to arrive with the news was a despatch rider sent by a gendarmerie outpost – and he arrived on his motor-cycle almost at the same time as the Germans on theirs. The main alert, however, came when Marquis was captured in bed at 4.30 a.m. and his staff were able to alert Labórde who was still naive enough to disbelieve, at first, that the Germans would attack the base. He ordered steam to be raised in all ships and for all precautions to be taken in case the Germans dare try to board them.

Five submarines got away while German troops were trying to scale the high walls and being shot at in the process. Then the order to scuttle was repeated again and again to all ships when an enemy tank bulldozed through the main gate. The French Fleet was about to honour its pledge.

Knowing that it could take up to five hours for most of the ships to work up sufficient steam to move out of the Inner Roads, the Germans were somewhat dilatory about their work and probably didn't know how quickly a ship could be scuttled. They were in the navy yard after 5 a.m., then it took another hour for the tanks and troops to find their way through the immense area to the larger ships moored at the outer piers. At last they reached the pier from which the *Strasbourg* had floated when her lines were cast off by the crew. Admiral de Laborde was aboard, as the Germans knew by now, and a tank fired an 88mm shell into a secondary battery turret, mortally wounding an officer. The German officer in charge called out to Laborde to hand over his ship undamaged but the admiral, who had ordered the ship's machine-guns to cease firing at the tank, replied that the *Strasbourg* had already been scuttled. The ship, and its sister ship, *Dunkerque*, took a lot of water to sink their 26,500 tons displacement and they sank slowly once the sea cocks were opened.

A German called out, "Admiral, my commanding officer sends word that you have his greatest respect," just before any further chit-chat was drowned by the sound of explosions from all parts of the ship: guns were blown up, important machinery was wrecked with hand-grenades, and oxy-torches burned through turbine reduction gears. Slowly she settled, on an even keel, to the bottom, and even then the large tower, reminiscent of the skyscrapers on Japanese battleships, was almost entirely out of the water.

The cruiser *Algérie* (full load displacement 13,900 tons) had been extensively overhauled at Toulon and was berthed two piers away from *Strasbourg*. The cruiser's sea cocks were opened and she was going down fast when a German hailed her to announce that he had come to take her. This was Admiral Lacroix's flagship on which he was going the short distance down. He informed the German that he was a little late, that she was already sinking. The German had heard and seen the destruction of her guns yet stated that he would go aboard when the Admiral told him that the ship would not blow up, whereupon the Admiral said that if the German did come aboard it would certainly blow up. A few minutes later the after turret blew apart. *Algérie* burned for two days with occasional eruptions as ammunition and torpedoes exploded.

From the high hills around the bay the people of Toulon, and the German troops stationed there, were provided with flame and fireworks display for more than a week, the time it almost took for the *Marseillaise*, an 8,214-ton (empty) cruiser of the sleek and fast *La Galissonnière* class, to burn herself out after settling on an angle. The latter ship was also scuttled, then she was salvaged and used by the Italians until retroceded to the French in 1944.

Not only did the "*Suffren*" class cruiser *Colbert* sink,

she blew apart when her magazine blew up, almost taking with her some of the enemy who had rushed on board then quickly off when they saw the fuses burning and an officer setting alight to his aircraft on its catapult. The same near miss among the Germans happened on the cruiser *Dupleix*. The battleship *Provence*, 22,000-ton sister ship to *Bretagne* and *Lorraine*, was almost lost to the enemy by the doddering indecision of her captain who was confused by a message: "Orders have been received from Monsieur Laval that all incidents are to be avoided." With other ships listing, exploding, settling and capsizing all over the place the captain thought he should follow suit although he was surrounded by armed Germans on his ship. He stalled for time by sending an officer across the yard to find out what the order actually meant, at the same time as his crew were pulling out the plugs. The captain and the Germans were still arguing and waiting for the officer to return when the old battleship slowly listed under their feet. The captain was led ashore smiling.

Dunkerque ended as scrap metal stripped away by Italian dock workers and sent back to Italy to be used in war material. Her guns had been blown up and turbines destroyed as she lay in the large drydock. Of the "2,100-ton" type large or "super" destroyers, three of them, *Lion*, *Tigre* and *Panthère* were staffed only with skeleton crews because of repair work; thus they were only partly sabotaged and they went more or less intact to Italy with the destroyer *Trombe*.

The *Strasbourg* had probably reached the bottom when Laborde, high and dry on the projecting upper works, was refusing to leave his ship, declaring to his German captors that they had broken their oath in encroaching on the French Fleet at Toulon. The German commander left him there, having theoretically gone down with his ship, until Pétain could persuade to him to leave his ship; and when he sent the signal, "I learn at this instant that your ship is

131

sinking. I order you to leave it without delay. Philippe Pétain,'' it was picked up by French naval units in North Africa, giving them their first news of the scuttle or whatever was happening to Laborde and his battleship.

The submarines *Venus*, *Casablanca*, *Marsouin*, *Iris* and *Glorieux* started instantly the alarm was given and as soon as crews could get to action stations; they had probably often practised for this scramble. Before German tanks could rush their pier they were on their way to crash through the booms with their strong, sharp bows. The commander of the *Glorieux* replied with pistol fire to the machine-gun fire from tanks and infantry. The anti-submarine net was withdrawn by its tender and when they passed through that barrier the submarines came under shell fire and a bombing and depth-charge attack by the Luftwaffe. Also, the exit channel had been mined. They certainly were going to the "gates of Hell," as the captain of the *Iris* called out to the captain of the *Venus*. The latter boat was damaged and, to facilitate an easier rescue of the crew, she was scuttled in the outer roads; *Iris* escaped and, for some unknown reason, her captain took her to Spain and internment – perhaps his idea of Heaven.

The other three submarines that escaped made it safely to Algeria while the four left behind at Toulon were scuttled at their moorings and their crews, like all other personnel at Toulon, were interned until it was decided what to do with them. The French successfully argued that the scuttling had not been an act of hostility, only an act of destruction legalised by the terms of the 1940 armistice so they were all released and continued to receive their regular pay from Vichy, as indeed, the dependents of Free French sailors also received their allowances from the same source!

*

Field Marshal Kesselring, commander of Luftflotte II and overall chief of the German forces in the Mediterranean, had been prepared for any eventuality in his area, whether Allied landings in North Africa, Sicily, Italy, Sardinia or southern France. The Italian navy he considered useless as a guarantor of sea transport safety so he sent parachute battalions and infantry by air, using Blohm and Voss seaplanes, JU-52's, JU-290's, Ghiblis, Savoia-Marchettis and enormous Me-323's to carry the men on their two-pronged attack against the British in Tunisia. The Germans landed at and near Bizerte and on the shores of the Gulf of Tunis, landings which were rapid and efficient, and developed later with such force that the British were held as they approached from Algeria.

On 27th November the German Admiral Weichold called on Admiral Derrien, commander of the Bizerte naval forces, to inform him that German troops were occupying Toulon, an action, he said, to prevent the French Fleet from sailing to North Africa. He asked Derrien to give an assurance that his ships would not attempt to escape, an impossibility anyway since the Germans held all approaches to the harbour, and Derrien believed that the terms of the 1940 armistice would be complied with. Derrien told his ship commanders, therefore, that he was confident the Germans would not attempt to seize the ships. A few days later those ships which had not been hit by Allied bombardment were still afloat, a small force but useful to the enemy.

On 8th December, the German General Gause handed Derrien an ultimatum to surrender immediately to the Germans all ships, shore batteries, depots and installations at Bizerte. Otherwise, he said, all French ships and troop barracks would be attacked by his circling aircraft; no quarter would be given to any of the crews or garrison troops; and since Marshal Pétain had, three days previously, acceded to German demands to disband French troops everywhere, Gause would consider all French troops and sailors to be

133

outside the military laws which applied to men in uniform.

Derrien felt that he did not have the right to send hundreds of men to their death simply to save his personal reputation, and he yielded to the ultimatum, sending this order to all ships and shore establishments:

"I have just learned from the German authorities that total demobilization has been ordered in France. In accordance with the terms of this order, the ships, batteries, depots, harbour installations, radio stations, and other military installations, as well as all small arms, must be turned over intact to the German and Italian troops. The troops of the Axis have taken all necessary measures to suppress forcibly and without mercy any attempts to resist, or to destroy, or to scuttle. I ask all officers, petty officers, soldiers, and sailors to obey this distressing demand in order to avoid useless bloodshed. This order is to be carried out without delay."

The vessels handed over to the Germans included 9 submarines, a damaged heavy destroyer, a small tanker, a minelayer and several small surface vessels – two sloops and three torpedo boats, the last five all later sunk when sailing under German or Italian flags. Two submarines were sunk during an Allied bombing raid the following month and just before the Allied troops entered Bizerte, two more were scuttled; three submarines were towed to Italian ports where they were eventually destroyed by retreating Germans before the boats were ever serviceable enough to go to sea. The ninth boat, *Phoque,* was repaired and joined Italy's navy only to be sunk by Allied planes before she could make a successful mission.

*

So ended the last symbol of France's national sovereignty, and gone too was the only thing the French had to bargain with the Germans in the 1940 armistice: it suited them both then – the Germans because it would mean that France could preserve her empire which the Germans would not want until they had defeated Britain, the French because they possessed a strong weapon that could be given to the Allies should the armistice terms be broken.

In December, 1942, Churchill at last heard direct from Darlan why Britain did not receive the French Fleet at the fall of France. The Admiral wrote: "If I did not consent to authorise the French Fleet to proceed to British ports, it was because I knew that such a decision would bring about the total occupation of Metropolitan France as well as North Africa. I admit having been overcome by a great bitterness and a great resentment against England as the result of the painful events which touched me as a sailor; furthermore it seemed to me that you did not believe my word. The voluntary destruction of the Fleet at Toulon has just proved that I was right, because even though I no longer commanded, the Fleet executed the orders which I had given and maintained, contrary to the wishes of the Laval Government."

Chapter 10

THE MURDER OF ADMIRAL DARLAN

*"Prime Minister hopes blame will be
placed on Germans and their agents"*

THE canny Churchill was quick to make sure that General
Eisenhower knew his political tricks when Admiral Darlan was assassinated, or murdered – there is a distinction:
if the perpetrator of the act kills for a personal reason it
is murder, if for political reasons or because he is a "hired
gun," then it is assassination. Anyway, the "Little Fellow",
the Admiral whom everybody except Pétain hated, was
shot dead while on his way to keep an appointment with a
BBC correspondent who had flown out to interview him in
Algiers. The time was Christmas Eve, 1942, when there was
no longer a "Vichy Fleet."

Short, tough, aggressive, Darlan looked as though he
could easily have got a part as a cop or a gangster in American movies. He was Churchill's *bête noire* among the
Vichy French, yet among his own countrymen in North
Africa he was more favoured as a leader than General
Giraud who had made such a spectacular escape from a
Nazi prison. Giraud was the Allies' choice as unifier and
leader and when General Clark suggested that Madame
Darlan take her son to America for treatment, he added, "I
think it could be arranged for Admiral Darlan to go, too, if
he chooses." That offer had more politics in it than concern for Darlan's feelings, which Darlan astutely noted: "I
would gladly turn this thing over to Giraud," he said. "He
enjoys it here. I don't."

Whether he knew it or not, he would be facing a charge

of treason by the Gaullists at the end of the war – possibly before – a fate that was to be Admiral Esteva's, among other naval officers. Esteva was responsible for Tunisia and, when the Germans invaded, Clark asked Darlan to order Esteva to resist the invasion, thereby proving Darlan's good faith. But Darlan had been sacked as Admiral of the French Fleet by Pétain, replaced by Admiral Nogues, and he told Clark that although he was not certain that any orders issued by him would be obeyed, he was sure that his old order to scuttle the Fleet rather than be seized by the enemy would be followed. Nevertheless, he tried to use his influence both on Esteva and Laborde, writing this to the latter:

"The armistice is broken. We have liberty of action. The Marshal being no longer able to make free decisions, we can, while remaining personally loyal to him, make decisions which are most favourable to French interests. I have always declared that the Fleet would remain French or perish. The occupation of the Southern coast makes it impossible for Naval forces to remain in Metropolitan France. I invite the Commander-in-Chief to direct them towards North Africa. The Americans declare that our forces will not encounter any obstacles from Allied Naval Forces."

That had as much influence as his efforts to have Esteva order Derrien into action, although Esteva was keen enough. After Darlan telephoned him, he issued this order: "After two days of talk and confusion, the order has just reached me explicitly designating the enemy against whom you are fighting. The enemy is the Germans and Italians. Soldiers, sailors, airmen of the Bizerte defences you now have your orders – blaze away with all your heart against the foe of 1940! We have a reckoning coming. Long Live France!" When Darlan telephoned to see what effect the order had produced, Esteva spoke with a German at his side.

The other fate that Darlan avoided was Esteva's in 1945 – sentenced to life imprisonment on a charge of collaborating with the Germans at Bizerte. That strange French handicap – Honour – was still working. Darlan may have suffered Admiral de Laborde's fate and been condemned to death for scuttling the fleet at Toulon. Like many others condemned, Laborde's sentence was commuted to imprisonment, the fate of Auphan, Marquis and Abrial, and many of the sentences were reduced. Esteva was released after five years and he died at home.

*

"Uniting the French is the matter of first importance. If it takes place around me, so much the better. But my person is of little importance. That it takes place is in itself the essential thing." A few hours after saying this in a broadcast, Darlan was dead.

The murderer, a young man named Fernand Bonnier de la Chapelle, was, according to General Clark's opinion, an unbalanced Gaullist; an official statement on the night of the murder suggested that it was of German or Italian inspiration; De Gaulle in his memoirs points to "a policy resolved to liquidate a 'temporary expedient' [as Roosevelt referred to Darlan] after having utilized it"; and Admiral Cunningham, closer to the truth, expressed an opinion that "many hands were in it, and it was of no service to the Allied cause."

Darlan had no delusions about his position and what the Allies, especially Churchill and de Gaulle, thought of him. "I am, perhaps, only a lemon which the Americans intend to throw away after squeezing it," he wrote to General Clark, and although the Americans did not throw him away he was destined for disposal once the intrigues in North Africa were sorted out and the renewed ally established with a leader favourable to all. He knew this and was fatalistic about his being used: "When the restoration of French sovereignty shall have become an accomplished fact, I will return to civil life. If this is what President Roosevelt means by 'temporary expedient', then I am in complete agreement."

He did not favour de Gaulle as a Saint Joan of Arc image to bring the French people into concerted action, or even as "the bride" to "the husband" (General Giraud) – as those two were referred to by Churchill and Roosevelt. Darlan was most likely correct when he expressed the unpopular opinion that it was still the men in France – Noguès, Boisson and Michelier as well as Giraud that the French in Africa could unite in confident cooperation "with the Allied armies and with the people of European France." The task of accomplishing that union, Darlan said, would be made more difficult if the Allies themselves created doubt among the French. The Americans were not happy with de Gaulle early in their association with him and in 1942 Roosevelt proposed that the General should be excluded from the Free French National Committee being installed in Algiers. Early the following year Churchill was to write to Roosevelt that he did not know what to do with the Frenchman who was so terrible to get on with. "Possibly you would like to make him governor of Madagascar," he said, adding that the General had a "Messianic complex". The letter, recently published by the State Department in Washington, also included this bit of intimate gossip: "If only they knew what you and I do about de Gaulle himself, they [the French people] would continue to be for the movement but not for its present leader in London." De Gaulle was to get his own back – on everyone, including Britain and America, while helping to inspire France to get back to normality and then on the way to a prosperity never known before.

Naturally, there were many people involved in everything political that happened in Algiers and North Africa during those awkward days of part French-Allied alliance, the greatest fuss being created by the problem of French leadership. American plotting had begun as early as 1940, through an Embassy man named Robert D. Murphy who became Counsellor at Vichy after the armistice. Roosevelt was one of the originators of the plan to land in North Africa and he transferred Murphy to Algiers where he could establish liaison with General Weygand who was the Delegate of France. Weygand was getting on in years when the First War ended and although he was sprightly enough in 1941 to pander to his odd quirk of vaulting over conference tables, he was really too old to be an active revolutionary leader. It was known that Darlan, "Popeye", as the Americans code-named him, was closely associated with right-wing pro Franco-German alliance organizations but after Japan thrust America into the war, and "Popeye" could add American might to Russian might – especially when the Germans failed to reach the Russian oilfields – he became pro-Allied. The French Underground refused to deal with him, Churchill despised him, and the Americans welcomed him. Among his many intrigues, Darlan was in touch with the head of the Abwehr Intelligence, Admiral Canaris, through an ex-head of an extreme right-wing French organization – the *cagoulards*, a ruthless lot.

They might all be compared with rats leaving a sinking ship, rats none the less who could be used as temporary expedients. During 1941 America sent food, cloth and oil to North Africa (winning friends among both French and Arabs) as well as intelligence officers. A useful conspirator during the following year was Jacques Lemaigre-Dubreuil, another with long association with right-wing groups, who became a member of the "Five"; the others were Rigault, d'Astier de la Vigérie (a staunch Gaullist), Colonel van Ecke and Tarbé de Saint-Hardouin. General d'Astier's Jesuit chaplain, the Abbé Cordier, kept the plotters' secret papers in a convent on behalf of Rigault. The Five recruited others to their cause without aiming too high among the top brass of the services, except in the case of Murphy's friend Weygand.

The Gestapo was already on the trail of the sprightly old man, who was becoming too popular with the Allies, according to their interpretation of Allied propaganda, and when a German general was taking back from North Africa a dossier on Weygand the plane was sabotaged, on Darlan's orders it has been suggested, and the inquisitor was killed. Weygand, however, was recalled to Vichy; in any case he probably did not care much for the type of people trying to make him a rebel. One important recruit was Brigadier-General Béthouart, commander of the Casablanca Division in Morocco. The Five were much more interested in friendship with the United States than with Britain, a good reason for giving the Torch operation a large display of American flags, even on the British destroyers which charged the harbour booms in Algiers. And the Five were not informed of the date for the operation or the fact that half the strength would be British.

To the Five, de Gaulle was not a popular choice as leader but Giraud was, and when he escaped from the French generals' prison, the high fortress of Koenigstein, he was soon met by Murphy and Lemaigre. This was the second escape Giraud had effected: in the First War he had been captured by the Germans and escaped with the help of nurse Edith Cavell – whom the Germans later executed. Giraud was all for starting the rebellion in France where he was to remain until after the North African landings, meanwhile appointing General Mast as his Chief of Staff in Algiers where he had already been appointed divisional commander by the Vichy Government, a useful post for a rebel. Thus Giraud was the choice of Lemaigre and the Americans, and Lemaigre insinuated that de Gaulle was a British puppet. "The African Army," he said, " on the whole disliked the British. Too much blood had been shed fighting them at Mers-el-Kebir, in Syria and at Dakar. All of this may have been necessary for the British, but it was humiliating and costly to France." Unfortunately there was much truth in this, a fact that made difficulties between the British and de Gaulle when American attitudes and wishes regarding the French were involved.

So the most outstanding anti-German leader was unpopular because he happened to be using a British base and British support and material aid in his fight to kick the Germans out of France, whereas most of the leaders in North Africa were suspect in the eyes of the untainted de Gaulle. Eisenhower later wrote that the streams of information received from American consuls and officials in Africa led him to believe that except with the very few Resistance elements among the civilian populations, de Gaulle was not popular and that "in the regular officer corps of the French Army de Gaulle was, at that time, considered a disloyal soldier".

When Churchill applied himself to the problem of French leadership he may have thought of the successful Anglo-American alliance and that de Gaulle should share control with Giraud. Meanwhile, Murphy had been conspiring with Darlan who had once told Admiral Leahy, US Ambassador to Vichy, that "I, Darlan, will be ready to march with you" if the United States landed a mighty force at Marseilles. Was it possible that, after all, the villain – in British eyes – would be the leader of North Africa's French, and later possibly of France? To many it was unthinkable yet to the French it was logical and probable: he was popular with the Navy and might win the support of the Army although General Mast told Murphy that negotiations could not be carried on with "a rival who could not be trusted".

Throughout all of this Mediaeval-type drama, there were many interwoven conspiracies which have been explained more fully elsewhere and are too lengthy for this work, but another man must be mentioned: General Bergeret, a young airman who also served in the Vichy Government's Air Department, and who was to become involved in the affairs at Algiers.

As already mentioned, it was Darlan who was on the spot when the Allies landed – not Giraud, who was delayed getting across to Gibraltar and where, for some reason, Eisenhower at first refused to talk to him.

*

When the huge Allied assault began Darlan cunningly played both sides until he was convinced that the Allies were capable of landing in force and establishing themselves in such strength that the Germans would not be able to dislodge them. Once that situation was reached he was in a position to say to the Americans that he commanded the obedience of the French. Indeed, armed with a secret message from Pétain authorising him to act as he thought fit, he was head man in Algiers and Murphy was forced to acknowledge his powerful influence as far as ending the fight was concerned. General Barré was his man in Tunisia, General Noguès in Morocco – both Vichy men too – and his influence was greater than the Allies' man in Algiers – General Juin. In that city the Admiral was able to see for himself that long lines of marching Americans were evidence of local success, and from reports of action in other areas he quickly decided to offer to arrange a cease-fire.

Back in Gibraltar the escaped Giraud was asking what would people think if he wasn't immediately appointed Commander-in-Chief of the whole Allied operation – probably with Eisenhower as his chief of staff. When he arrived in North Africa he fatefully accepted his soldier's duty to accept Darlan as his superior. Needless to say, the Resistance members complained about Darlan's position to Murphy who said that he could do nothing about it. Too many unexpected events had happened, there were too many pressures and there was a war going on all around them as the actors in this weird drama visited one another in hotels and military establishments.

The most important thing was the successful prosecution of the war. For the Allies, Darlan could have continued as Commander-in-Chief of the French forces despite the fact that he was continuing to follow orders from Pétain at Vichy. Darlan had signed the armistice document with General Clark, an act which forced Pétain, who was forced by the Germans, to disavow the Admiral, whereupon his morale collapsed as if he'd suddenly been declared not to be a Frenchman: he asked Clark to make him a prisoner of war!

"That's OK by me," said the amazed American, who soon afterwards agreed to release the "prisoner" who had decided that since the Germans were now in the unoccupied zone, breaking their armistice agreement, he was again free to help the Allies. It was the old French *honneur* syndrome at work again with many situations occurring whereby *honneur* could be adjusted to suit the most beneficial. It affected Juin: because Pétain, he reasoned, was virtually a prisoner and as there was an old rule that no French soldier could take orders from a captured officer thus he was free from his oath to the Marshal; then another *honneur* obstacle cropped up when his Corps commander Koeltz said that Juin's orders were no more legal than Darlan's. Thus the French did not resist in Tunisia and the Allies were given an extra burden of a campaign in that country. It was time to throw all the Pétain men into a compound yet Clark again insisted on keeping Darlan as the figurehead when Giraud developed a spirited liking for the position.

Noguès was the next to arrive, full of Vichy loyalty which was without too much enthusiasm to fight Germany, and as far as he was concerned there was *no* General Giraud. Next came the British Commodore Dick from Admiral Cunningham who had been told by Churchill: "If I could meet Darlan, much as I hate him, I would cheerfully crawl on my hands and knees for a mile if by so doing I could get him to bring that fleet of his into the circle of the Allied forces.'' Alas, that fleet was now diminished. And then the Gaullists were told by Darlan where de Gaulle stood in the new scheme of things: nowhere. Darlan appointed the Five to his Cabinet; the airman Bergeret as his deputy; d'Astier and Rigault as heads of the police forces of North Africa. It should have been obvious to the Admiral that the Allies were not at all interested in restoring France to a Vichy clique or in relegating to obscurity the head of the Resistance movement; more obvious was the fact that Darlan was the centre of a dispute with strong pressures coming from all sides. Perhaps he hoped to become president. He already possessed a liking for pomp: his personal train in France was equipped with two bathrooms and wherever he travelled he was accompanied by a twenty-four piece orchestra.

By the middle of December, Darlan had been long enough in the new political scene to realise that he must accept de Gaulle if the General would cooperate with him; the General wouldn't. D'Astier and others invited the Pretender to the French throne, the Count of Paris, to enter the scene so that he could become a temporary head of the Council – not as the Pretender but as a French citizen – and so ease out Darlan peacefully. The Count lived in a large villa in Morocco, for pretenders were not allowed to live in metropolitan France, and he was driven up from his eunuch-staffed, bizarre residence, travelling in the car with the Abbé Cordier. The usual round of secret and semi-secret meetings were made with those whose approval was necessary, but when the plan was nearing fruition, Eisenhower refused to change the French leadership just when the Tunisian campaign was in a critical phase. If not by peaceful means, then by other means, plotted the anti-Darlan faction.

*

In London, where Churchill was able to review the war – which was swinging in favour of the Allies – with more confidence, de Gaulle was anxious to make contact with Giraud; the obstacle was that Darlan was refusing to allow de Gaulle representatives into Algeria. Churchill told the General that means of getting representatives out there would be placed at his disposal, thereby enabling d'Astier's Gaullist General brother Emmanuel, and Pierre Frenay, to fly to Algiers. When they arrived, Darlan ordered his police to arrest them and they were placed under surveillance at the Hotel Aletti. No doubt they would have gone to prison but for the presence of Henri d'Astier and the fact that Ike was now in Algiers, a presence conducive to saner negotiating. Full of Gaullist enthusiasm, Emmanuel d'Astier upset the Allied C-in-C by refusing to talk to Darlan until, after much persuasion by Murphy and others, he agreed to do so the following night. Apart from a couple of insults, nothing came of the meeting with Darlan and Giraud who went later that night to Eisenhower's house, asking him to send d'Astier away.

The following day, 21st December, Darlan heard that the Free French emissary intended to visit Morocco and Dakar, news that spurred Darlan to order him out of the country and North Africa. Emmanuel, by now thick with Gaullist plotters, refused to leave until he had gathered a mass of information on the North African situation. He left for London two days later, the day Darlan gave a luncheon for Allied Naval and Military leaders; afterwards he told Murphy, who attended the luncheon, "You know there are four plots in existence to assassinate me. Suppose one of these plots is successful, what will you Americans do?" It was the kind of statement one would expect to read in a history of the Roman emperors.

At 3 p.m. the following afternoon Admiral Darlan and his aide, Captain Hourcade, entered the offices of the High Commissariat in an old Moorish pavilion. In the antechamber was a young man who had filled out a request to see a Monsieur Joxe. Suddenly, as Hourcade passed the young man, a shot rang out, then another, and Hourcade turned to see Darlan slumped on the floor at the entrance to his office. The aide grappled with the gunman who shot him in the neck and thigh before getting through a window in an effort to escape; there a Spahis cavalryman caught him. Darlan was dead on arrival at the hospital to where he had been rushed in a car. When the murderer, Fernand Bonnier de la Chapelle, was hit by twelve bullets from a firing squad, he was twenty years old.

Darlan's murder was an opportunity for all the factions to lay accusations against each other, all of them rushing into secret discussion and inquiry. Clark immediately insisted on Giraud taking over the reins of government, and, before the truth came out, the US Secretary of War, Henry L. Stimson, announced that arrested suspects must be Vichyite or pro-Axis, adding that he had been impressed by the wisdom and loyalty of Darlan. The main suspects of course were Gaullist and among those arrested were two who were charged by members of the Deuxième Bureau as the main instigators and who were accused by their associate, André Achiary:

"I accuse two persons of being the direct instigators of the murder of Admiral Darlan: they are: the Abbé Cordier, and Henri d'Astier de la Vigerie, Assistant Secretary General for Political affairs at the High Commissariat, both residing at number 2 rue Lafayette. These persons had Admiral Darlan assassinated on behalf of the Count of Paris who ... urged them to be quick about carrying out the crime ..."

Commissioner Garidacci was also arrested because he had withheld at the inquest a true confession made by the murderer who named the accomplices; in its place, Garidacci produced a second confession also signed by the boy stating that he had acted alone!

147

At his trial Bonner was reported by a police officer of having made a long statement to him in conversation, a statement that involved people by name and implication. He said that certain people had spoken to him of the fruitless attempt of de Gaulle's envoy to meet Darlan, and that they said "Darlan must disappear," so he decided to make him disappear. He mentioned that he knew the Count of Paris and d'Astier, and stated that "if the person for whom I made Darlan disappear did not take power, we would become Anglicised or Americanised; this for France's sake must not be" – true Gaullist philosophy. "My trial was no trial," he said, "there was no inquest. They accuse me of killing a man; well, on 8th November, General Noguès, in Morocco, had many killed for no reason, and Darlan did the same in Algiers . . ." That was true, for the General and the Admiral could have stopped the battle against the Allied invaders.

In the true confession which the cunning Garidacci had persuaded, posing as a friend, the boy stated that he affirmed killing Darlan "after having told the Abbé Cordier I would do so in the form of a confession. It was M. Cordier who gave me the plan of offices at the Commissariat and of the offices of the Admiral; it was through him I was able to obtain the pistol and shells which I used to execute the mission I had assigned myself . . ."

Bonnier expected to be saved from the execution squad but as the fatal hour approached he was still alone; in a panic he confessed his story about the Jesuit priest but the listening police thought he was raving.

In January, at Casablanca, Churchill and Roosevelt attended the "wedding" of Charles de Gaulle and Henri Giraud, and the only real smile seen in the group photograph was Churchill's.

*

Using typical sermon-like phrases, Historian Churchill wrote in his *The Second World War, Vol. II*, this obituary to Darlan: "The fame and power which he ardently desired were in his grasp. Instead, he went forward through two years of worrying and ignominious office to a violent death, a dishonoured grave, and a name long to be execrated by the French Navy and the nation he had hitherto served so well."

There is one thing certain: if the Gaullists hadn't killed Darlan, Special Operations Executive (SOE) agents would have done so.

It is doubtful if Darlan's grave has ever been dishonoured; it certainly was not at the time of his burial, for he was given a State funeral attended by a long procession, headed by Eisenhower, Cunningham, Clark and many high-ranking French, American and British officers and officials, followed by military detachments from all the Allied and French services. Bands played during the march and he was buried in a casement of the Admiralty at Algiers where French sailors maintained a constant vigil.

Chapter 11

ONCE MORE ALLIED

WITH the death of "Popeye" Darlan (or "The Lemon Drop Kid"), it was natural for the Allies to expect Admiral Godfroy to give up the good shore life in Alexandria and take his ships to sea. *Honneur*, or a defiance which had become constipated, kept 66,000 tons of valuable naval assistance tied up in the Egyptian bay until General Giraud sent the Admiral a letter of assurances that a reunion would be advantageous to France, a letter of flowery nationalistic phrases that included the words "generosity", "sincerity" and "tolerance". Two days after receiving the letter, on 17th May, 1943, Admiral Godfroy radioed Michelier, and of course Vichy, that he was joining the Naval Forces of Africa – which were now joined to the Allies.

Laval ordered him to scuttle his ships – too late, for Godfroy was committed, his ships were brought up to complement with sailors from Algiers and the main part of Force X – the battleship *Lorraine*, and the cruisers *Duquesne, Tourville, Suffren* and *Duguay-Trouin* – made a long shake-down journey around the Cape to Dakar. It was Godfroy's last voyage on his battleship; at Dakar he was relieved of his command and left idle until some months later he read in a newspaper that he had been compulsorily retired "as a disciplinary measure." The rest of his Alexandria holiday crowd sailed the submarine *Protée* and the destroyers *Basque, Fortuné* and *Forbin* to Algeria.

In Algiers, Giraud had adopted lower case when he remarked to the Naval District Commandant, "I do not like vice admirals." Nor was de Gaulle happy with admirals, for his old FFNF commander Muselier had left him and gone to Africa where Giraud appointed him to a post equivalent to a police commissioner, and when Muselier found the Gaullists inciting troops to desert to their ranks he considered placing de Gaulle under arrest. Before de Gaulle's French Committee of National Liberation took over the Navy, and before Giraud himself was forced to retire from the political and military leadership (and was lucky not to have been assassinated also) French workshops and American salvage groups worked hard to get the remnant Fleet back into working order. Altogether there were over a quarter of a million tons of shipping in the Navy, the bulk of it in North and West African ports.

Including the uncompleted *Jean Bart*, there were three battleships, an old aircraft carrier, three heavy cruisers, one auxiliary and seven light cruisers, five *contre-torpilleurs* (heavy destroyers), six destroyers, seven corvettes, two sloops, and nineteen submarines – 54 useful warships plus 84 mixed craft comprised of colonial sloops, minesweepers, MTB's, submarine chasers, river gunboats and patrol vessels.

The French already had their own radar although it was still rather experimental: the equipment installed on the battleship *Richelieu* at Dakar could pick up aircraft some fifty miles away, and a few other ships had been equipped with an improved radar before the Toulon scuttle. To bring the Fleet up to the improved Allied standards of 1943 the ships were equipped with radar, asdic and more powerful anti-aircraft guns.

While there were some clashes between the Pétainists and the Gaullists, officers and men were eager to fight the old enemies once the *barbaresque* Navy was free of the land-based squabbles and went to sea on active duty. Eventually the African ships were once more under the united title of Marine Nationale which also replaced the FFNF. As more Frenchmen joined the Navy more ships were given it by the Allies: during the next two years Britain handed back several ships, that could be spared, which had been seized in 1940, adding a Hunt class destroyer (*La Combattante*), six frigates, four submarines – including a captured Italian boat – and sixty-five other vessels; the United States provided six destroyer escorts, one hundred and seventy-two other vessels and forty landing craft – all in 1944; and from the Italians, when their country was invaded and forced to an armistice, the heavy destroyer *Tigre* was recovered along with the *Trombe* and a small aviation tender.

The greatest need was for escorts for numerous convoys around African waters and the Mediterranean where the smaller French ships could be of immediate service. Cruisers went out into the Atlantic to help British cruisers searching for raiders and enemy merchantmen and blockade-runners: the *Georges Leygues* sank the *Portland* on this duty. Enemy air action impressed on the French the importance of extra anti-aircraft guns and modern control equipment which was installed on some ships in America, the complex work of repair and modernization being effected in record time by the amazing American workmen.

The battleship *Richelieu* made the trip to the United States, as did several cruisers and destroyers. While the *Richelieu* was in the Brooklyn naval yard she was referred to by the New York press as being part of the "French Nazi Fleet". The ship carried a portrait of Pétain and the adverse publicity most probably stemmed from Gaullist agents who were busy enticing crew members of all French ships to the Gaullist cause. These disruptive tactics were ill timed; they were bad for morale, especially as the *Richelieu* was about to join the British Home Fleet at Scapa Flow. Admiral Andrew Cunningham and Secretary of the Navy, Frank Knox, were among those who denounced the disruptive tactics which were widespread – from Algiers to the Antilles.

Once they were in power in Algeria and the other French

territories when they were reoccupied, the Gaullists were often misguided in what can only be described as vicious activities. Vice-Admiral Derrien, the Bizerte commander, had trumped-up charges, as well as the one of not scuttling his ships, laid against him. Chained and imprisoned in the old Foreign Legion jail at Maison Carée he became ill and was eventually released after the war on a suspended sentence. A few days later he died and was given a funeral with full military honours; it having something to do with *Honneur*, the thing denied him at his trial which was not, according to the rule, conducted by admirals but by an Army Tribunal. Another example was poor old General Barré, the first ex-Vichy general to take the field after the armistice and who led his troops to victory beside the Allies in Tunis, who was excluded from the Regular army. Again Roman history makes suitable comparative reading.

The story of the little islands of the Antilles, remnants from the days of French Canada, involves the 300 tons of gold taken there in 1940; the naval commander Admiral Robert who was also High Commissioner; an agreement with the United States covering such matters as warships and merchantmen, food supplies and blockade; and three political factions – Vichy, Gaullist and Communists, the latter two mostly indistinguishable. American influence won the battle against Vichy orders to scuttle and sink the gold, but it wasn't until July, eight months after the coup in North Africa, that a new administrator arrived on board the *Terrible* and took over from Admiral Robert who chose to return to HQ at Vichy and wait for his post-war trial. He served eighteen months in prison.

In the Antilles was the aircraft carrier *Béarn* which was sent to the old French possession, New Orleans, to be over-hauled and converted to ferry aircraft. The *Jeanne d'Arc*, designed as a training ship for midshipmen, was a useful cruiser; she was overhauled in Puerto Rico before taking part in the Allied operations at Corsica. Another cruiser

153

picked up in those islands was the fast *Emile Bertin* (almost 40 knots) but her repairs and modernising took so long the war was almost over by the time she was back in service.

*

Rear-Admiral Lemonnier was appointed Chief of the new National Navy's Operations with Rear-Admiral Auboyneau as his deputy; their headquarters were established at Algiers while their British command was administered by Louis Jacquinot, who was also appointed Minister of the Navy. Escort duty and submarine hunting were the main operations for the French, and their bases were most valuable in the European campaigns of late 1943 and 1944. After duty with the British Home Fleet, *Richelieu* joined the Eastern Fleet operating against the Japanese. French ships worked in the Dodecanese when British troops were landed on Kos and Leros Islands, and French submarines sank eight enemy ships during forty-five patrol missions; the submarine *Protée* was lost. Destroyers and submarines were extensively employed in the landings and later supplying of Corsica, an important French victory which gave the Allies space for seventeen airfields and a launching base for the landings in Provence.

At long last a mighty Allied armada was collected in British ports and adjacent waters to shepherd the D-Day force to its Normandy landings. The light cruisers *Montcalm* and *Georges Leygues,* the destroyer *Combattante*, eight frigates and corvettes, a flotilla of MTB's and some minesweepers were given the desirable honour of participating in the landings of 6th June, 1944. The two cruisers joined the battleship USS *Arkansas* less than a thousand yards off the coast at Port-en-Bessin, firing salvo after salvo against enemy batteries above the American landing sector.

German guns at Longue were silenced soon after they opened up on landing craft approaching the beach, shell fragments from the *Georges Leygues*'s broadsides blasting through casemates and killing enemy gunners.

Apart from a few commandos, no French troops were included in the Allied landings: there might have been a language difficulty, said the planners. However, during the few days the *Georges Leygues* spent on bombardment duty off the coast, a boat's crew went in with a British commando unit to meet the inhabitants of Port-en-Bessin. Meanwhile, *Combattante* lent her guns to the British assault near Courseulles and silenced a German shore battery. A few days later she carried de Gaulle when he made his first return visit to France. The other French naval units also played their parts well, escorting, running in with supplies and throwing up shell and tracer patterns against enemy aircraft. And, like a ghost from the French Navy's past, the old battleship *Courbet* was towed over from Southampton and sunk with other old ships to form a protective break-water at Ouistreham.

While that successful invasion continued, *Montcalm* re-fuelled, rearmed and victualled for her voyage out to the Mediterranean where she had an engagement with another invasion, one which was more sentimentally important to French sailors for it meant going back to their Toulon base and liberating the large port of Marseilles. If they had been asked, every French sailor would have volunteered to sail in the lead ship of the invasion.

Operation "Anvil" was a controversial decision, one favoured by Joe Stalin because he hoped it would keep Allied troops out of the Balkans where he intended to support Communist governments. Roosevelt's comment was that he saw "no reason for putting the lives of American soldiers in jeopardy in order to protect real or fancied British interests on the European continent," and favoured the operation endorsed at the Teheran conference where

Churchill was out-voted on the question. De Gaulle was satisfied with the arrangement although General Juin, commanding four French divisions in Italy, asked him to think again on a "most disquieting strategy." Quite realistically and sensibly he reasoned, as did the other Allied commanders in Italy, that an excellent opportunity existed to increase the pressure there and cross the Apennines to "roller-skate" down into France. Not only did Roosevelt believe in Stalin's veneer of goodwill, he had the elections at home to consider: even a slight setback in Operation Overlord might lose the election for Roosevelt, as he said in a letter to his "dear friend" Stalin, if it were known that "fairly large forces had been diverted to the Balkans."

The southern France invasion at least helped the northern operations, freeing more men to Eisenhower and holding many Germans from rushing north; and it enabled French troops to share in the spectacular invasion of Hitler's European fortress. There was a large proportion of colonial troops in General de Lattre de Tassigny's French divisions that formed part of the US 7th Army main force. De Lattre was not a Gaullist and had commanded the Montpellier area under the Vichy Regime; he had been imprisoned for planning to fight the Germans when they entered the unoccupied zone, managed to escape to England, and was appointed to his command simply because he was a very good general. When his commandos were about to land this signal was sent to them: "The Admiral, officers and crews of the Allied Fleet salute Lieutenant-Colonel Bouvet and his men, who will have the honour of being the first to set foot on their native shores, and to liberate their land. May God guard and protect them."

The strongest Allied naval defence preparations were for aerial attack: seven British and two American escort aircraft carriers were among the huge fleet supporting the landings. There were five French cruisers and three heavy destroyers lending their bombardment power to the bigger guns of the battleship *Lorraine*; other destroyers and smaller French warships were also engaged, convoying troops of the first French Army.

The biggest target for the bombardment ships turned out to be the guns from the scuttled battleship *Provence*. Two 340mm guns had been hauled up to the battery at Cape Cépet on the Saint-Mandrier Peninsula jutting out to form Toulon's large bay. Originally there had been two two-gun turrets in the battery which also received the scuttle treatment in 1942. Two of the guns had been repaired by the Germans, one of which was again sabotaged before the landings commenced, and before the *Lorraine* came up with her 340mm guns a complete turret of the shore battery had been knocked out in an air raid. In a short duel the battleship silenced the remaining gun.

The landings took place at several points – between Cavalaire and Saint-Tropez, Nartelle, between Agay and Saint-Raphaël, Cap Nègre, Levant Island and Le Trayas. Compared with Normandy it was a walkover and in some parts there wasn't any need for naval gun support. American rangers who landed on Levant Island to silence a battery discovered that the guns were made of wood and that there were no German defenders. The Germans were in strength, however, in the Saint-Raphaël–Issambres area and very sensibly those beaches were by-passed and the positions taken by flanking attacks. 1,200 ships had made almost an uneventful approach and two armies landed with comparative ease.

Toulon's enemy batteries provided target practice for Allied battleships and cruisers while de Lattre's troops attacked with a feint against the eastern side, then a major assault down from the hills in the rear. It was now the Germans turn to scuttle ships in Toulon's harbour; they attempted to scuttle the *Strasbourg* and *La Galissonnière* so as to block the southern channel but were foiled when American Mitchell bombers sank them; three U-boats and other craft went down from scuttling or bombing. While the German defenders were being driven back to isolated strong points, the American advance inland had taken them well on the way to Grenoble and the Rhône valley.

The strongest German point at Toulon was the Saint-mandrier area where the single gun from the *Provence* again came to life and again *Lorraine* and Allied big guns were brought to bear on it and silence it forever. Toulon itself was entered on the 25th August and the last redoubt fell three days later.

French and Allied ships moved along the coasts east and west towards Nice and Ports Vendres, operating parallel to the troops until by the end of the month the complete southern French coast was back in the hands of its rightful owners. And then much salvage work and mine-sweeping was carried out so that French warships, trailing their long action pennants and flying battle flags, could make their way into Toulon harbour.

*

Long before all the sailors could go home to begin their analysis of the war and its unhappy consequences. for Frenchmen, there were still those matters in the Far East to be attended to. Most of the French possessions were in the hands of the Japanese who were on the retreat through the Pacific in 1944.

The *Richelieu*, now with her after deck bristling with anti-aircraft guns, gave added protection to the aircraft carriers HMS *Illustrious* and USS *Saratoga* during bombing raids on Sumatra and other Japanese targets at Sabang. She silenced batteries on the island of Pulo-We and then went back to Casablanca and Gibraltar for a long overhaul. In April, 1945, she went back to the Far East war, with the battleship HMS *Queen Elizabeth* to Sumatra and the Andaman Islands; she sailed out to attack a Japanese cruiser and was bringing her guns to bear when the cruiser went down as the result of a daring torpedo attack by British destroyers, a frustrating attack for Captain Jean du Vignaux, for it was his last opportunity in the war to test his ship's prowess against an enemy warship. Returning from South Africa where her bottom had been cleaned, *Richelieu* arrived at the Trincomalee base in Ceylon when the war ended. She was scrapped a few years ago.

Of the small French Fleet in Indo-China only two gunboats, *Frézouls* and *Crayssac*, escaped the Japanese at Haiphong and managed to reach the China coast; there they barely survived by paying extortion to both Chinese troops and pirates; at the war's end the ships returned to duty at Haiphong, helping other French warships and French troops re-establish authority over a land which has not experienced total peace from then until now.

In the period between the ending of the Third Republic which lasted from 1870 to June 1940, and the end of the war, the French Navy was in action against German, Italian, British, American, Japanese and between its own warships; it was reduced in size from one of the largest fleets in the world to one of the smallest, yet its critics – if they have any understanding of human nature – must admit that the friendless fleet emerged from the Second World War with its *honneur* intact, and that despite its vicissitudes and prolonged idleness, it survived with a record of courage and some notable achievements.

BIBLIOGRAPHY

Papers at the Public Records Office, London.

The French Navy in World War II, by Auphan and Mordal. (US Naval Institute)

The Trial of Marshal Pétain, by Jules Roy.

Pierre Laval, by Geoffrey Warner.

The Murder of Admiral Darlan, by Peter Tompkins. (Weidenfeld & Nicholson)

1940 The Fall of France, by General André Beaufre. (Cassell)

The Second World War, by Winston Churchill. (Cassell)

History of the Second World War. (Purnell)

The War in France and Flanders, by L. F. Ellis. (HMSO)

The Naval War 1939-1945, by Captain S. W. Roskill RN. (Collins)

Wings of the Morning, by Ian Cameron. (H & S)

Grey Gladiator, by George H. Johnston. (Angus & Robertson)

A Sailor's Odyssey, by Viscount Cunningham. (Dulton)

Fighting Admiral, by Donald Macintyre. (Evans)

My Three Years with Eisenhower, by Harry C. Butcher. (Heineman)

Calculated Risk, by Mark Wayne Clark, (Harrap)

War Memoirs, by General Charles de Gaulle. (Collins)

Diplomat Among Warriors, by Robert D. Murphy. (Collins)

Sept fois sept jours, by Emmanuel d'Astier de la Vigerie, (Guild du livre)

Sixty Days that Shook the West: The Fall of France, by Jacques Benoist-Mechin. (Jonathan Cape)